FIERCE
RESILIENCE

FIERCE
RESILIENCE

(Combatting
Workplace Stress
One Conversation
at a Time)

EDWARD BELTRAN

BK

Berrett–Koehler Publishers, Inc.

Berrett-Koehler Publishers, Inc.
1333 Broadway, Suite P100
Oakland, CA 94612-1921
Tel: (510) 817-2277
Fax: (510) 817-2278
bkconnection.com

ORDERING INFORMATION

Quantity sales. Special discounts are available on quantity purchases by corporations, associations, and others. For details, please go to bkconnection.com to see our bulk discounts or contact bookorders@bkpub.com for more information.

Individual sales. Berrett-Koehler publications are available through most bookstores. They can also be ordered directly from Berrett-Koehler: Tel: (800) 929-2929; Fax: (802) 864-7626; bkconnection.com.

Orders for college textbook / course adoption use. Please contact Berrett-Koehler: Tel: (800) 929-2929; Fax: (802) 864-7626.

Distributed to the US trade and internationally by Penguin Random House Publisher Services.

Berrett-Koehler and the BK logo are registered trademarks of Berrett-Koehler Publishers, Inc.

Printed in Canada

Berrett-Koehler books are printed on long-lasting acid-free paper. When it is available, we choose paper that has been manufactured by environmentally responsible processes. These may include using trees grown in sustainable forests, incorporating recycled paper, minimizing chlorine in bleaching, or recycling the energy produced at the paper mill.

Library of Congress Cataloging-in-Publication Data

Names: Beltran, Edward, author.
Title: Fierce resilience : combatting workplace stress one conversation at a time / Edward Beltran.
Description: First edition. | Oakland, CA : Berrett-Koehler Publishers, Inc., [2024] | Includes bibliographical references and index.
Identifiers: LCCN 2024004698 (print) | LCCN 2024004699 (ebook) | ISBN 9781523007141 (paperback) | ISBN 9781523007158 (pdf) | ISBN 9781523007165 (epub)
Subjects: LCSH: Job stress—Prevention. | Psychology, Industrial.
Classification: LCC HF5548.85 .B45 2024 (print) | LCC HF5548.85 (ebook) | DDC 158.7/2—dc23/eng/20240411
LC record available at https://lccn.loc.gov/2024004698
LC ebook record available at https://lccn.loc.gov/2024004699

First Edition
32 31 30 29 28 27 26 25 24   10 9 8 7 6 5 4 3 2 1

Book production: PeopleSpeak
Cover design: Ashley Ingram

To Susan for believing in me and our vision for bettering the world one conversation at a time.

CONTENTS

FOREWORD

The Japanese have a word—*karoshi*—that can be translated into "overwork death." It is very real, can be sudden, and is not uncommon. While you may not be in danger of keeling over at your desk, based on results, what doesn't kill us does not make us stronger. It makes us anxious, struggling to cope with persistent worry and apprehension.

The good news and the bad news are the same news.

The good news is that your doctor can prescribe one of fifty-four medications currently available for anxiety, and just about every smartwatch out there can detect serious health risks, such as atrial fibrillation, respiratory issues, and stress levels.

The bad news is that your doctor can prescribe one of fifty-four medications currently available for anxiety, and your watch can tell you that you're stressed.

The problem is taking a pill and receiving alerts from your watch don't tell you why you are anxious, much less how to resolve the anxiety. Although we are prompted to exercise, meditate, stop smoking, and change our diet, anxiety persists.

If the pharma and tech worlds have invested considerable dollars, time, and effort in alleviating anxiety, it must be a big deal. It is. Roughly 301 million people worldwide are taking a pill for anxiety. Companies consider the mental health of their employees a top priority. It's a no-brainer that anxiety is a productivity killer and a career saboteur. Plus, if you care about your employees, you want them to be happy, healthy, and resilient.

If we all felt less anxious and more resilient, that would be wonderful, but how in the world do we achieve this? Well, if you're tired of filling yet another prescription for anxiety or worrying that your blood pressure is higher than it should be, and you would like to replace your anxiety with resilience, the answers are in this book.

In *Fierce Resilience: Combating Workplace Stress One Conversation at a Time*, Ed Beltran provides the solution. Since our bodies don't lie, Ed worked with experts in the field of biometrics to take the proven principles and practices of Fierce Conversations, which are backed by years of expertise in managing workplace dynamics, into the world of science, providing biometric intelligence via an app called Pulse for your wearable device that does far more than alert you to stress signals.

First, Pulse is like a tiny stress detective for your life. It uses the latest stress-tracking science, pairs up with your wearable tech, and—this is *huge*—connects stress events to your calendar so you can see exactly *when* you are stressed: for example, when you are giving or receiving feedback, leading or attending another waste-of-time meeting in which you suspect the real issue is not on the table, dealing with a difficult client, reviewing your to-do list (which you know to be impossible) with your boss, confronting poor performance, and more. Now you can connect the dots: *"This is when I feel stress. This explains another sleepless night."*

Second, Pulse provides tailored advice on navigating your stress. If, for example, you are stressed when you need to give feedback, the app offers AI coaching to give you tailored approaches on what to do the next time giving feedback is on your schedule. You'll learn an approach to providing feedback that changes a potentially stressful event into a productive conversation that not only gets the job done but also enriches the relationship.

You will understand that your career, your company, your relationships, and your very life succeed, flatline, or fail gradually, then suddenly—one conversation at a time. It seems we are often asleep during the "gradually" part of our lives, only waking up when we arrive at a devastating "suddenly," such as a serious illness, the loss of a job, the loss of a relationship, the loss of confidence and happiness. Now you can intervene in your own mental health during the gradually, heading off an unwelcome suddenly. And while no single conversation is guaranteed to change the trajectory of a career, a company, a relationship, or a life,
any single conversation can.

Ed provided Pulse to individuals and organizations before offering it to the world, and the feedback has been a huge aha. The theme that self-awareness + Fierce Conversations = sustainable resilience was a home run.

To say that I am thrilled about this is an understatement. It has been deeply gratifying to work with Fierce clients worldwide and celebrate their amazing results. It is wonderful to receive emails from individuals who tell me the huge difference these conversations have made in their companies, marriages, and lives.

Best of all, Pulse is available to you 24/7. You'll have Fierce in your pocket, so to speak. No more anxiety. You will be resilient.

—Susan Scott, Author
Fierce Conversations, Fierce Leadership, and *Fierce Love*

PREFACE

I was a young adult when the immensely popular book *Fierce Conversations*, authored by Susan Scott, came out. Having even good conversations wasn't on my radar. But fierce conversations sounded like something to be avoided at all costs. I didn't think much about the impact of my words. I wasn't searching for clarity and understanding. I would have laughed at the idea of emotional intelligence. None of this was on my radar at all.

I was focused on the same goals as most young people: getting an education, starting a career, having fun, finding love. To be honest, I wasn't fierce or resilient. But I was driven. I had built a strong foundation of finance, technology, and business skills that took me through major consultancies as an adviser to large corporations and start-ups. I experienced the high levels of stress that come from working in high-powered organizations. Welcome to adulthood.

My mentors and managers had beliefs that contradicted the principles of authentic communication. They taught me to hide vulnerabilities, keep information close, and manipulate situations for personal gain. However, I was at a breaking point while working as the head of finance in a multibillion-dollar company. I blamed the president of the organization for the cultural and performance issues but later realized that I played a significant role in perpetuating these problems in my capacity as a leader of multiple teams.

Fed up with my situation after four years, I sought new opportunities in Seattle and stumbled upon Fierce, an organization I had never heard of before. Its mission of bettering the world one conversation at a time, despite often being referred to as *soft skills*, piqued my interest.

Discovering the book *Fierce Conversations* was transformative. Through easy-to-grasp conversation models, it empowered me to handle interpersonal issues in both my personal and professional life. My life was profoundly changed, especially considering my background in large, impersonal corporations where incivility was the norm.

When I read Susan's book, one phrase hit me hard: "What conversation or conversations did you miss or fail at to get you to this point?" I personally was stunned by her ideas. They changed me as a leader. They made me deeply reflect on my career and life, realizing that my success or failure often hinged on the quality of my interactions and, more importantly, my ability first to recognize when difficult interactions were necessary and then find the courage and skill to engage in those interactions. I realized that I had missed opportunities.

One incident that came into sharp focus was when the CEO of my previous company told me I was responsible for influencing better outcomes, especially when working with the president. At the time, I didn't listen to the real message. As I read Susan's book, it dawned on me that the CEO's statement was not just a request but a requirement for me as a senior leader, and it wasn't about me. Unfortunately, I failed to meet that expectation, and the CEO who had hired me held me accountable for my ineffectiveness. I had failed at that important conversation. I now understand the importance of authentic conversations and how they shape outcomes and relationships.

I joined Fierce, a company started in 2001 by Susan, who has also written *Fierce Leadership* and *Fierce Love*. Her principles became the training engine for millions of people.

With Susan's blessing, I was appointed chief executive officer and have worked to implement a shared vision of the future, bringing in new ideas, technology, and talent to further the mission and impact of bettering the world one conversation at a time.

I work closely with a wonderful team that includes Gabe De La Rosa, who serves as our chief behavioral science officer. Gabe's expertise is in industrial and organizational psychology research, making him one of the navy's top combat and stress experts. His research focused on resilience and how people and organizations stay aligned with their mission by combatting stress.

My own background and love of technology, Susan's extraordinary perspectives, and Gabe's research helped create a new platform called Fierce Resilience and a new application called Pulse. Our team merges high-tech solutions designed to improve workplace culture and create the resilient workforce needed for the future. Our shared passion is making a difference in the world by alleviating stress in the workplace. To do this, we use an approach more focused and—as our research is indicating—more effective than traditional stress-management techniques, all while driving extraordinary outcomes.

I am thrilled to share our knowledge and insights to help individuals and organizations build Fierce Resilience—a mindset and skill set to tackle stressors, engage in effective communication, and thrive in the face of challenges. This book is designed to demystify stress and take a radical approach to resilience, one that doesn't suggest resilience is only for the gods among us but instead presents a model where anyone can learn to become more resilient and build organizations that have resilience as a core part of their DNA. The key to building Fierce Resilience is to predict, understand, and overcome the stressors that challenge work and personal lives. Fierce Resilience has become integral to how I lead my life, and I'm honored to share it with you.

INTRODUCTION

Fierce Resilience: Combatting Workplace Stress One Conversation at a Time helps create a culture of resilience, empowers teams, and transforms companies by dramatically reducing stress in the workplace. Throughout the book, I will emphasize the importance of having the courage to become self-aware and act by becoming attuned to your body and conversations. It is about thinking and acting fierce.

This book is aimed at people who are part of any type and size of workplace: in-person, hybrid, or virtual. At times, I specifically address issues and responsibilities of leaders, but most of my views are pertinent to everyone who is part of an organization. Additionally, while I only address a few non-work-related challenges with stress, the ideas and models used definitely apply to personal and family life.

I will share personal anecdotes, case studies, exercises, practical guidance, and actionable strategies that have been used at Fierce Inc., where I am CEO. In stories, vignettes, and most case studies, I have used first names to signify pseudonyms. In a few instances where I deemed it important, I have used full names to indicate real people.

The book is divided into two parts, and I strongly recommend reading part 1 to understand the principles and research behind my recommendations. Part 2 includes specific ways to overcome some of the top stressors individuals and organizations face.

Part 1, "Understanding Fierce Resilience," describes the Fierce Resilience Cycle, the four key steps to achieving Fierce Resilience: awareness, analysis, assessment, and action. I redefine resilience, draw inspiration from elite athletes, explore the relationship between workplace stress and resilience, and rethink traditional approaches to stress management. I also introduce the power of self-awareness, the role of biometric intelligence in fostering self-awareness, and how an innovative tool that my team at Fierce and I created supports individuals on their journey toward resilience when coupled with skillful, structured conversations and traditional stress-management techniques.

Part 2, "Practical Applications of Fierce Resilience," will show you how to put it all into action by using several conversational models to address common challenges faced by organizations. The Fierce Resilience Cycle provides practical strategies to put into action. The goal of this section is to help you do the following:

- Positively create an optimum workplace culture
- Effectively give and receive feedback
- More easily overcome conflict
- Feel more comfortable when working outside your comfort zone
- Navigate an improved work and life balance
- Respond to change with calm and confidence
- Handle high-pressure conditions through a unique approach to delegation

Join me on this transformative journey as we embark on a quest to alleviate workplace stress one conversation at a time. Together, we can build Fierce Resilience, empower individuals and organizations, and create workplaces where individuals and organizations build collaborative cultures based on constructive interactions, leading to desired results.

PART 1

UNDERSTANDING FIERCE RESILIENCE

CHAPTER 1

REDEFINING RESILIENCE

It is not the most intellectual of the species that survives; it is not the strongest that survives; but . . . the one that is able best to adapt and adjust to the changing environment in which it finds itself.

—LEON C. MEGGINSON

I constantly think and talk about resilience. It started at a young age. My Mexican grandmother, my *abuela*, was a tough cookie who acquired her toughness surviving the Great Depression. She grew up very poor, working in the fields as a child and as a domestic as an adult, while raising eight kids in a two-room shack. She always kept her head up and lived every day with esteem and pride in her work. We joked that she would clean to the zealous extent of sweeping dirt off dirt floors.

My abuela prized what she had. Facing many obstacles, she remained mentally tough, never complained or felt sorry for herself, and continued working every day. One of my earliest memories, from when I was five or six, is of walking with her to the eastside San Jose parks and digging through garbage bins for aluminum cans to recycle for money. She saved that recycling money for me to attend college.

I didn't grow up poor like my abuela, and the money from those cans was unnecessary for my college fund. But the lessons she was teaching me were necessary. We can see the value in and be grateful for everything. When times are tough, we can always find an answer if we're willing and humble enough to grab for it. And most importantly, physical toughness is not enough. My abuela gave me my first lessons about resilience. She was one fierce woman.

These lessons have followed me into adulthood and my career. As the CEO of a global leadership-development and training company, I delved deep into how structured conversations improve workplaces. I became particularly fascinated with the concept of resilience, how it relates to stress, and why structured conversations and biometric intelligence yield remarkable results for individuals and organizations. Biometric intelligence assesses how your body reacts to your environment to drive deep self-awareness of the whats and whys, moving you to actions that tackle tough stressors and challenges. Together with a team of experts, we created and patented a device that helps gain insights about your body's reaction to stress and connects it with data relating to the events that are causing stress. The result has been millions of people building Fierce Resilience and combatting stress one conversation at a time.

To start the conversation about resilience, I'd like to share some history about the concept. I am a person who likes to cut to the chase, so I'm going to first reveal the spoiler—the definition I have ended up with after lots of experience and research:

Fierce Resilience is the courage to self-assess and act.

This definition may seem deceptively simple, but it embodies three important elements. First, it acknowledges that resilience takes courage. That's one reason I have modified it with the word *fierce*. You have to be brave to become resilient. You aren't born with this quality. You have to exercise your resilience muscle and often work outside your comfort zone.

Second, it requires self-awareness. Too often, we take a Band-Aid approach to problems such as stress and congratulate ourselves on being resilient. In truth, most of what we experience is misplaced stress because we avoid getting to the root cause, which identifies what specific challenge you need to address and what acute stressors need to be dealt with.

That's where self-awareness comes in. We now have technology that lets us become more aware of our bodies' reaction to stress. That means we don't need to guess why we are feeling stressed. Our bodies tell us through biometric intelligence. We become aware in the moment.

Third is the word *action*. Too often, people believe that if they understand a problem, it will go away. Or they apply traditional stress-management tools that are useful but don't get to the root cause of their stress—the relationship they have with others and themselves. I have found building resilience requires more direct and proactive action. Sustainable Fierce Resilience is created when you learn how to have healthy conversations based on different situations. That's where action comes in.

A clear way of visualizing these ideas is with the Fierce Resilience Cycle shown in figure 1.1, which will be used to guide you through this book.

Before I dive deeper into this, let's start by looking at the history and context of a word that gets you more than one billion hits if you type it into a Google search engine—resilience.

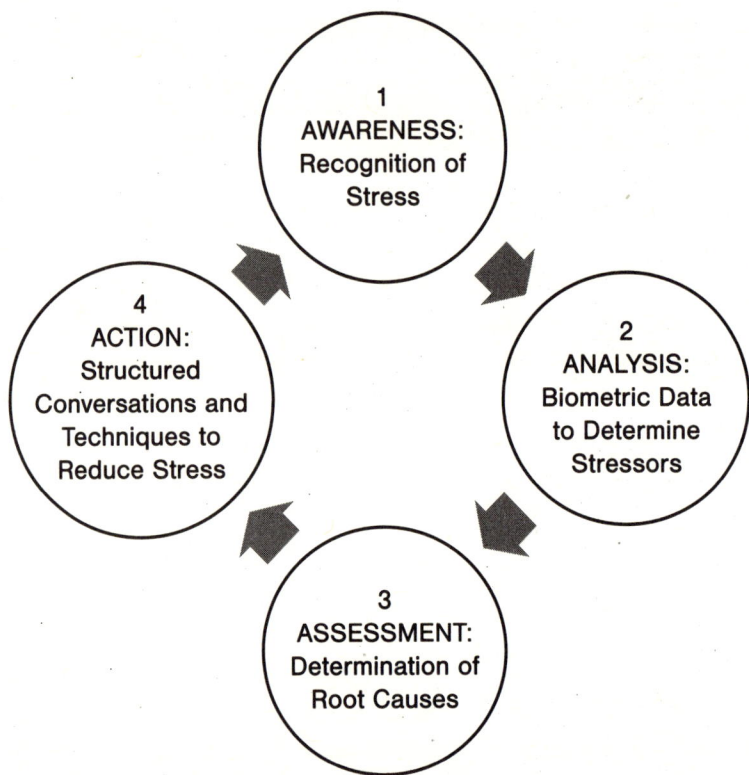

Figure 1.1. The Fierce Resilience Cycle
Source: Fierce Inc.

WHAT'S IN A WORD?

Here's a definition from the *Oxford English Dictionary*:

re · sil · ience
/rəˈzilēəns/
noun

1. the capacity to withstand or to recover quickly from difficulties; toughness.
   "the remarkable resilience of so many institutions"

2. the ability of a substance or object to spring back into shape; elasticity.

"nylon is excellent in wearability and resilience"

> *Similar:* flexibility, pliability, elasticity, springiness, ability to last, strength of character, hardiness, adaptability, ability to bounce back
>
> *Opposite:* rigidity, fragility, vulnerability, weakness

The word *resilience* came into the English language in the seventeenth century, when we needed to describe the ability to bounce (in Latin, *salire*) back (the prefix *re-*) from a disruption or attack. With the discovery of rubber, resilience came in handy to describe that material's physical property of bounciness or elasticity. A resilient material stretches when stressed but rebounds to its original form.

D. E. Alexander explored the history of the term as it evolved from the purely physical to more metaphorical applications to describe the bounce-back abilities of communities and ecological systems. He wrote, "The first serious use of the term *resilience* in mechanics appeared in 1858, when the eminent Scottish engineer William J. M. Rankine (1820–72) employed it to describe the strength and ductility of steel beams" and then "how mechanics passed the word to ecology and psychology, and how from there it was adopted by social research and sustainability science."[1]

RESILIENCE BOUNCES INTO THE TWENTY-FIRST CENTURY

By the 1980s, we started to use the word *resilience* to describe a person's, community's, or system's ability to recover from trauma or stress. This abstract use of the word deals with concrete, real-world problems. Additionally, global organizations launched campaigns to build resilience in communities, economies, and governments. A resilient community retains its cohesion in times of disaster and upheaval. A resilient economy finds ways of surviving financial crises. A resilient government responds to the stresses of social change by reorganizing according to the needs of its people.

RESILIENCE GETS PERSONAL

Psychologists then took the ball and ran with the concept of resilience on the personal and psychosocial levels. The *European Journal of Psychotraumatology* surveyed the scientific definitions and ongoing research and found that most proposed definitions for resilience included "a concept of healthy, adaptive, or integrated positive functioning over the passage of time in the aftermath of adversity."[2]

The experts agreed that resilience may be defined differently in the context of individuals, families, organizations, societies, and cultures. Scientists reached a consensus that resilience studies require levels of analysis, including "genetic, epigenetic, developmental, demographic, cultural, economic, and social variables."[3] They recommended that resilience-building programs be tailored to individual or community-level definitions and the variables they identify.

The American Psychological Association created its own definition: "Resilience is the process and outcome of successfully adapting to difficult or challenging life experiences, especially through mental, emotional, and behavioral flexibility and adjustment to external and internal demands."[4]

Resilience: a concept of healthy, adaptive, or integrated positive functioning over the passage of time in the aftermath of adversity.

Let's step away from the experts for a few minutes and illustrate the idea of resilience through two areas that have played a role in my life: comics and sports.

RESILIENCE IN THE MULTIVERSE (COMIC-BOOK WORLDS)

I love superheroes and so do my kids. They reflect so much of our worldview. That made me curious about how resilience plays out in the multiverse. According to Superpower Wiki, the power to bounce can be applied for enhanced durability or invulnerability, enhanced leaping, and impact absorption.[5] You see this superpower in comic-book heroes from the birth of comics onward.

Plastic Man from vintage DC Comics has the superpower of elasticity, stretching, bounding, shape-shifting, and bouncing back to his resilient original form. Mr. Fantastic, also known as Reed Richards, is a founding member of the Fantastic Four in Marvel Comics. As a result of exposure to cosmic rays, he gains the ability to stretch his body and limbs to incredible lengths and is always able to bounce back. Elongated Man, a DC Comics superhero, also has the power of elasticity. Like Plastic Man, he can stretch his body and limbs to great lengths. Elongated Man's powers also grant him enhanced agility and durability. And some of you may identify with Marvel's Wolverine, whose superpower is his resilience: he is haunted by PTSD and the attacks of his archenemies, but he has the power to heal from all assaults and go on to the next challenge.

Fierce Resilience enables us to bounce back from stress, but it does more. Empowered by self-awareness, the fiercely resilient person identifies the sources of stress and then confronts and defuses them. It enables us to bounce forward, taking our organizations to new levels of effectiveness. That's where assessment and action in the Fierce Resilience Cycle come in. If comic books make their superheroes resilient, then humans might yearn for that super-power too. Elite athletes know that well.

ELITE ATHLETES PRACTICE RESILIENCE

As an amateur athlete, I have been intrigued with the ability of elite athletes to achieve amazing feats powered not just by physical prowess but also by the mental ability to meet challenges, bounce back from discouragement, and forge a path forward. They know how to grow their game out of both success and failure. They have trained themselves to a superhuman physical and mental resil-ience level. One great example is Bethany Hamilton.

It was just another day in paradise. But for Bethany, this day would bring her face to face with the scariest carnivore in the ocean. Surfing with friends at Tunnels Beach, Kauai, Bethany was attacked by a massive shark. It came up from the murky depths, bit through her surfboard, and took off her arm—a surfer's worst nightmare.

But amid that terror and pain, Bethany kept her composure, keeping her alive long enough to get to the hospital. She lost more than half of the blood in her body, but if she had panicked, her heart would have worked harder, and she would have bled out a lot faster. She kept calm, allowing her friends to get her to the hospital so the doctors could save her life.

Bethany had acquired an understanding of Fierce Resilience: accept the inevitable wipeouts. She made the commitment to rehabilitation with the goal of getting right back in the water. She learned to adapt to living and surfing with one arm. After her wounds healed and she had built up her strength, she got back on her surfboard, inventing creative, adaptive ways of using balance and buoyancy to stay afloat and ride the waves with one arm. And she learned to accept the inevitable wipeouts.

Bethany had buoyancy. She had resilience. Her physical comeback wouldn't have been possible without the mental and emotional resilience that powered her rehab.

AMATEURS HAVE RESILIENCE AS WELL

As a kid, I would act out and get in trouble, especially in high school. When I lost a fight or was "acting like a fool," my father always said, "Get your butt into the gym." I returned to the gym to beef up, but what gave me the cojones to get back there? What did I learn from those workouts that empowered me to get back into the fray reenergized?

I learned resilience requires both body and mind. Kicking my butt back to the gym, I learned what elite athletes have been practicing forever: mind-body resilience. The gym workouts built my strength, but I was also building mental resilience. Working out was meditative and got me back to my core. My time in the gym created the mental space to look inward and build self-esteem to handle any problem.

Today, I use those skills as an avid road biker, cycling one hundred to two hundred miles a week year-round. What better place to find your center and connectivity to spirituality than on a forty-to-fifty-mile ride with nothing but you, your bike, your thoughts, and the elements? My dad was right about getting tough, but I needed more than physical toughness. I needed to clear my mind, clarify my goals, and empower myself by getting holistically resilient: body, mind, and soul. My time in the gym created the mental space to look inward.

Resilient elite and amateur athletes teach us that resilience is a physical regimen *and* an attitude. A regular physical regimen will get us back in the gym despite injury or loss. Adopt an attitude that relishes the process of learning from both failure and success. Discipline is not just a motivation but the discipline of the mind. *Fierce Resilience requires both body and soul.*

RESILIENCE RESEARCH STUDIES? YES, IT'S A THING!

Let's look at resilience from a historical perspective. By 2014, enough research had been done to merit a survey examining what resilience meant in a wide range of fields, including psychiatry, medicine, management, education, military training, and global development. Researchers found some variables identified with resilience are "positive self-esteem, hardiness, strong coping skills, a sense of coherence, self-efficacy, optimism, strong social resources, adaptability, risk-taking, low fear of failure, determination, perseverance, and a high tolerance of uncertainty."[6]

Corporate trainers also were working with the resilience concept, applying it to keep us all sane and functional in the face of workplace stress. Workplace resilience studies look at all levels of the corporate organization chart, including the resilient employee, the resilient team, the resilient CEO, and the resilient organization.

Common themes across resilience studies in leadership training include the concepts of hardiness and recovery from adversity and the stages of survival, recovery, and thriving.

HARDINESS AND THE FOUR Cs

Many resilience models are founded on the hardiness concept, first developed in Suzanne Kobasa's 1979 article in the *Journal of Personality and Social Psychology*.[7] As resilience studies moved into the corporate world, Salvatore Maddi and his team at the University of Chicago applied Kobasa's work to research workplace resilience. In their book *Resilience at Work*, Maddi and Deborah Khoshaba defined the three Cs of hardiness: commitment, control, and challenge.[8]

Maddi and his colleagues developed their theory of hardiness through their work with Illinois Bell Telephone (IBT) back in the '80s.[9] Deluged with employee stress during a traumatic period of deregulation and downsizing, IBT engaged Maddi's team to study the characteristics of the employees who bore up most success-fully under those stressful conditions. They found that two-thirds of the IBT workforce failed miserably: employees experienced heart attacks, strokes, substance abuse, obesity, poor performance reviews, demotions, depression, and divorces.

We haven't improved decades later. We are warned about these outcomes on a daily basis and told that we need to change our diet and exercise more or meditate. These are all good ideas, but they are not enough because they don't get to the cause and resolution of our stress.

The one-third of the workforce that managed to thrive all had in common the attitudes of commitment, control, and challenge. They were committed to staying engaged in the process, not iso-lated on the sidelines. They committed to owning the elements of the change process that were in their power to control rather than standing by passively as the company went through its changes. And they faced the challenges of those difficult times as opportunities for learning, growing personally and professionally, even while two-thirds of their colleagues were defeated by the challenges.

Here's what the three Cs of hardiness look like in resilient people:

- *Commitment* means staying committed to your goals and never giving up.
- *Control* means that you believe that you are in control of the important tasks and events in your life. When stressful situations arise, you feel confident and act.
- *Challenge* means you see a rough road or stressful situation as a challenge to be faced courageously. When you embrace challenge, you accept change as natural. You see stress as an opportunity for growth.

Maddi and his Hardiness Institute later added a fourth C: connection. *Connection* emphasizes the importance of community in supporting individual and organizational hardiness and resilience.

WHAT'S MISSING FROM THE FOUR Cs?

One C that did not make it into the hardiness model is *conversation*. My work with Susan Scott and Fierce Conversations has clearly validated the importance of conversations. Susan believes that the next frontier for exponential growth for individuals and organizations lies in the area of human connectivity. She believes that those who can connect at a deep level with the people important to them at home and at work will take the field and hold it as well as experience more joy and health, mentally and physically. And this connectivity happens one conversation at a time. For me, this is the secret sauce and the core of the critical action step in the Fierce Resilience Cycle.

Specifically, Fierce Conversations are the ability to have structured conversations based on practicing self-awareness and discovering root causes. The quality of our conversations equals the quality of our relationships. I will spend a significant amount of time in the upcoming chapters and particularly in part 2 talking about conversations and how they are essential to Fierce Resilience.

For now, think of a Fierce Conversation as one in which you come out from behind yourself into the conversation and make it real. That takes courage and commitment to the organization and your own personal processes of continual improvement. Making the conversation, and therefore relationship, real requires an attitude of control over how you choose to face the challenges. The strength of the conversation is the strength of the relationship.

BECOMING FIERCE

Perhaps nothing has tested our resilience in recent times more than the COVID-19 pandemic. People experienced enormous impacts on their mental health, with anxiety and depression skyrocketing. Yet experts were also surprised that most individuals showed resilience. They were able to bounce back from COVID-induced stress and learned strategies to use at home and work.

But the truth of the matter is that stress in the workplace has always been a problem. According to prepandemic data from the Anxiety Disorders Association of America, up to 72 percent of American employees said stress and anxiety interfered with their day-to-day lives. Additionally, 40 percent reported persistent stress or excessive anxiety linked to their jobs, and 28 percent reported experiencing job-related anxiety and panic attacks.[10]

The COVID-19 pandemic sent already problematic workplace stress levels soaring, and its aftermath—particularly economic uncertainty—is still creating stress-inducing situations that affect workplace productivity, communication, and interpersonal relationships.

Until now, resilience training has focused on building an individual's inner resources. But that view of resilience makes the recipient of stress the victim, leaving the source of stress still out there, lurking in the shadows, ready to strike again, which necessitates a recurrent cycle of stress and recovery. Since the source of stress is often in human relationships and interactions—real or perceived—we needed to find a way of resolving those challenging relationships.

Fierce Resilience is a process of growth for the whole organization, starting with individual self-awareness. As Susan Scott writes about Fierce Conversations, "Doesn't 'fierce' suggest menacing, cruel, barbarous, threatening? Sounds like raised voices, frowns, blood on the floor, no fun at all. In *Roget's Thesaurus*, however, the word 'fierce' has the following synonyms: robust, intense, strong, powerful, passionate, eager, unbridled, uncurbed, untamed. In its simplest form, a Fierce Conversation is one in which we come out from behind ourselves into the conversation and make it real."[11]

CASE STUDY: A FIERCE VICTORY

Victoria is a formidable force as the CEO of a thriving staffing company. She is known for her intelligence, tenacity, and unwavering determination. Under her leadership, her company has grown exponentially, but with the expansion came an intense amount of everyday stress that weighed heavily on Victoria's shoulders.

Inside the walls of her office, Victoria struggled with the mounting pressure, relentlessly juggling tasks and facing critical decisions. Her personal life suffered, too, as the stress followed her even outside of work.

Victoria strongly believed that resilience was the key to facing this stress head-on. She embraced the idea of resilience, determined not to let the challenges break her spirit. Instead of succumbing to the pressure, she channeled her inner strength to confront each obstacle with unwavering determination. She refused to be defeated.

She realigned parts of her organization. She prepared intensely for potentially confrontational meetings. She adjusted her personal life, making time for joy, nurturing her passions, and spending cherished moments with loved ones. She tried stress-management strategies, such as meditation.

Nothing quite worked. "I guess I just don't have that resilient gene," she told herself. Then she talked to one of her mentors, who suggested redefining how she looked at resilience. Instead of seeing resilience as a character trait that one either has or doesn't, she should look at it like a muscle that would be strengthened using the right tools, starting with self-awareness of her stressors.

TAKING RESILIENCE FURTHER

Gabe De La Rosa, our chief behavioral science officer, leveraged his decades of experience and research in dealing with stress, building resilience, and optimizing performance in both military application and civilian workplaces. His research clearly shows that having Fierce Conversations lowers stress and drives resilience for the individual and organizations. These bottom-line impacts come from people engaging in structured conversations that enrich relationships, clear up misunderstandings, and add clarity to organizational objectives.

Let's look at this in simple terms. Millions of interactions happen in our companies and across the world hourly and daily. Think about the statistical probability for misunderstanding from failed delivery by the sender, a listening or processing error by the receiver, or both. This fact is well-documented. We as individuals have a choice to engage these situations we face every day.

Have you ever walked away from a situation thinking, "What did that mean?" or "I should have said this" or "I have no clue what I'm supposed to do." Our research shows that 90 percent of the time these misunderstandings can be quickly rectified when we address them in a timely and appropriate manner. This is being Fierce.

We also see correlations with organizational objectives when this level of engagement occurs. And it just so happens our measurable stress levels drop an average of 10 to 15 percent and, in many cases, 30 to 40 percent. I'll share more on this later.

Now that I have redefined resilience, I invite you to join the conversation. In later chapters, I will talk about the following topics:

- How workplace stress works against organizational peace and productivity
- How to identify stressful situations
- Ways to use biometrics to measure and track stress responses
- Traditional approaches to stress management
- How Fierce Conversations overcome stressors

TAKE A MOMENT

Let's take a breather to make what I am talking about more relatable to your own life. Try answering these three questions:

- Where in your life experiences have you shown resilience?
- What was the situation?
- What did you do to combat the stress?

Let's flip this:

- Where in your life experiences have you failed to show resilience?
- What was the situation?
- What was the result?

RESILIENCE REFRESHER

- The Fierce Resilience Cycle is a four-step process to combat stress through awareness, analysis, assessment, and action.
- Fierce Resilience is the courage to self-assess and act.
- The conversation is the relationship. Fierce Conversations defuse personal and professional relationship stress.

CHAPTER 2

THE RELATIONSHIP BETWEEN WORKPLACE STRESS AND RESILIENCE

Now he won't let go of the shovel,
and he can't dig out of the hole.

—RANDY TRAVIS, "THE HOLE"

Taro, age thirty-one, was found dead at his workstation. Cause of death: cardiac arrest. Cause of cardiac arrest: cumulative stress due to pressure to perform under a torrential workload, embedded in a corporate culture that preaches, "Just take it. Don't complain. And don't dream of talking about it."

The Japanese have a word for this: *karoshi*. It means "death from work." It happens a lot and not just in Japan.[1] In 2016, the World Health Organization found that, globally, 745,194 deaths were attributed to the stress of overwork, along with 23.3 million daily adjusted life years lost to ischemic heart disease and stroke.[2]

First responders in New York, Los Angeles, and other municipalities know that job stress causes heart attacks. Any police officer who has a heart attack either on or off the job is automatically compensated for a work-related injury, even if the event occurs while fishing on vacation or gambling in Las Vegas.[3]

WHAT'S STRESS?

If you ask a physicist, they'll tell you that when a deforming force is applied to an object, the object deforms.[4] To bring the object back to its original shape and size, an opposing force must be generated inside the object. This restoring force will need to be equal in magnitude and opposite in direction to the applied deforming force. The measure of this restoring force generated per unit area of the material is called *stress*.

Take note of that idea of a restoring force. It's the superpower of resilience.

Moving from physics to the human world, stress becomes harder to define. It's a state of anxiety or tension caused by a difficult situation, and different situations stress different people. You feel stress in response to situations that you perceive as dangerous or overwhelming—"threats to homeostasis," as biologists would say. We each have our personal stress triggers, so one person's stressful situation might be another person's cakewalk. Muscles tense up, heart rate increases, the mind races in circles, and in the work context, perhaps people scope out another job.

Stress: a state of anxiety or tension caused by a difficult situation. Different situations stress different people in different ways.

But studies have found that the job type isn't intrinsically stressful but rather the worker's attitude in relationship with the task and work environment.[5] For example, police officers, whose jobs have been called hyperstressful, surprisingly report they're more stressed by their paperwork than by chasing bad guys on the street.

I found one survey particularly interesting regarding resilience in the workplace. In 2014, researchers Sarah Bond and Dr. Gillian Shapiro asked 835 employees from public, private, and nonprofit firms in the United Kingdom about what drains their resilience in workplaces.[6] Economic challenges or the pace of change did not make the list. Instead, they answered that the biggest drain on resilience was relationships.

Imagine! Three-quarters said that the biggest drain on resilience was "managing difficult relationships/politics at work." Pause here and take that in—75 percent! That was followed closely by stress brought on by overwork and by having to withstand personal criticism. In fact, everything on the list relates to stress that is alleviated by using the Fierce Resilience Cycle.

REMOTELY DIFFERENT?

You would think that remote workers might report less stress than those still embroiled in the frying pan of the workplace. But no. What determines stress, rather than *where* they work, is how the employee feels in the organization. Workers who feel more engaged and involved feel less stressed.

That's not to say that the stressors are the same for remote workers and those in the office. The level and kinds of stress experienced while working from home or in an office vary significantly depending on individual preferences, job roles, and specific circumstances. No one-size-fits-all answer exists as different people may find different work environments more or less stressful.

Working from home provides greater flexibility in managing one's schedule and environment, which can reduce stress for some individuals. However, working from home also leads to feelings of isolation and loneliness, especially if there's limited social interaction or support. Home environments may have more distractions, such as family members, pets, or household chores, which impacts productivity and increases stress.

Office-based work often involves a daily commute, which is stressful due to traffic, public transportation delays, or long travel times. Interacting with coworkers and managers is both positive and negative, depending on the work culture and relationships in the office. Workplaces also have distractions, such as office chatter or interruptions from colleagues, which may hinder productivity.

Ultimately, the stress level associated with either option depends on individual personality traits and attitudes, the nature of the job, the work environment, and the level of support and flexibility offered. Some people may thrive in a home office environment, while others may prefer the structure and social aspect of working in an office.

WHAT ARE STRESSORS?

Let's look at the concept of stressors. Surprisingly, the term isn't that old. It was introduced by a physician named Hans Selye in 1936.[7] He observed significant changes in lab animals when they were subjected to certain stimuli, such as bright lights or loud noises. If these conditions persisted, it led to chronic illnesses in the animals. While the term *stress* gained popularity, its meaning has been somewhat fluid over the years. Many associate it with the fight-or-flight reaction our bodies have in response to adverse situations. But that doesn't encompass the entire scope of how stress impacts us.

The World Health Organization offers a comprehensive definition: "any type of change that causes physical, emotional or psychological strain. Stress is your body's response to anything that requires attention or action."[8]

UNDERSTANDING STRESS RESPONSES

Stress, traditionally viewed as a result of negative events, is better understood as any event or interaction that prompts an internal physical reaction. These reactions manifest in several ways, such as an increase in heart rate, breathing, and blood pressure; decreased heart rate variability (HRV); and a rush of chemicals through the body, which enhances awareness and alertness, leading to diverse emotional responses. Table 2.1 shows the behavioral, psychological, and physiological signs of stress.

We need to recognize that stress is not exclusively rooted in negativity. In fact, many life events, including those that are exciting or surprising, also generate stress reactions. By viewing stress as a multifaceted response to various life events, we broaden its definition beyond mere negative connotations.

The stress response is both natural and unavoidable in our lives. Ideally, this response functions akin to a wave. It begins when an event necessitates our response, making us alert and energized to handle the challenge. Once the situation is managed, we should ideally return to a restful mental state, recuperating from the event's effects.

In essence, stress serves a significant purpose: it acts as a signal indicating that something critical requires our attention and action. You can equate this to the Check Engine light of your mental health. The unease accompanying stress should ideally propel us into action to mitigate this discomfort. The key lies in recognizing that not all stress is detrimental, and we should be able to differentiate our personal stressors from those affecting others. I will help you learn this skill.

In the meantime, take a few moments to assess your own stress by asking yourself these questions:

Table 2.1. Signs of stress

Behavioral	Psychological	Physiological
• Having trouble sleeping or feeling tired all the time • Avoiding tasks or people you are having problems with • Eating more or less than usual • Drinking or smoking more than usual • Feeling irritable, impatient, or wound up • Being unable to enjoy yourself • Feeling uninterested in life • Losing your sense of humor • Procrastinating	• Racing thoughts or difficulty concentrating • Lack of self-confidence • Feeling of being overwhelmed • Sense of being neglected or lonely • Panic attacks • Sense of dread • Anxious, worried, nervous, tense, afraid or scared states • Depression	• Difficulty breathing • Blurred eyesight or sore eyes • Sleep problems • Fatigue • Muscle aches and headaches • Chest pains and high blood pressure • Indigestion or heartburn • Constipation or diarrhea • Nausea, dizziness, or fainting • Sudden weight gain or weight loss • Rashes or itchy skin • Increased sweat • Skin irritations • Upset stomach

Source: Fierce Inc.

- *Behavioral*—How does this impact the way I act in different situations?
- *Psychological*—What thoughts do I experience?
- *Physiological*—What physical responses do I experience?

UNDERSTANDING MICROSTRESSORS

Microstressors are like bees. While a single one might be a mere annoyance, a swarm poses a genuine threat. Often, the massive upheavals aren't what throw us off course but the accumulation of these tiny, unnoticed stressors that lead to feeling overwhelmed. The key to resilience is recognizing and addressing these microstressors before they escalate into significant stress episodes.

When we talk about stress, our minds often jump to significant, life-altering events, such as financial crises, job terminations, grave health diagnoses, or unexpected accidents. Psychologists call these types of events *traumatic stressors*. Recognizing this classification helps us differentiate between major events and the myriad of minor daily pressures.

Interestingly, many individuals navigate substantial crises with an impressive degree of resilience. These significant events, frequently broadcast in the news or experienced by acquaintances, have subconsciously prepared us to cope when adversity strikes. During these times, the strength of our community and social networks truly shines. For instance, following a massive tornado that devastated several areas last year, countless volunteers from across the nation rallied to assist in rebuilding, displaying the power of collective support.

However, as time progresses, it becomes clear that while we are often adept at overcoming major setbacks, we are susceptible to the cumulative weight of small, persistent stressors. These seemingly inconsequential pressures, often overlooked, accumulate, taking a toll on our mental well-being and leading to issues such as workplace anxiety and burnout. Moreover, a consistent buildup of these stressors not only affects our mental state but also manifests in physical symptoms, such as hypertension, sleep disturbances, weakened immune response, and digestive problems.

Addressing stress effectively means paying attention to the minutiae.

Addressing stress effectively means paying attention to the minutiae. *By managing the minor stressors, you prevent them from snowballing into overwhelming challenges, safeguarding both mental and physical health.*

As highlighted in a study from the *Harvard Business Review*, microstressors are subtle, often unnoticed stressors that impact our daily lives.[9] These stressors are categorized into three primary areas:

- *Impacts on personal capacity*—These stressors arise from our interactions at work or with others. For instance, feeling overwhelmed when unexpected tasks pile up or feeling restricted in how you perform your job causes stress.
- *Emotional reserves depletion*—These stressors stir negative emotions within us. They might emerge from confrontational discussions or encounters with pessimistic individuals. The constant brunt of such interactions wears down our emotional well-being.
- *Identity and values challenges*—This category involves stressors that make us question our self-worth, push us to go against our principles, or upset our social dynamics. For example, someone could be undermining our confidence or situations might force us to go against our core values.

While many of us might brush off these microstressors as just a part of life, we need to understand their cumulative effect. Regularly facing these stressors without addressing them erodes our resilience. To maintain our well-being, we must learn to recognize these daily stressors and find ways to manage or mitigate their impacts.

Let's chat about self-awareness. Think about it: we all have pet peeves. We might know how to make our friends roll their eyes or laugh, sometimes just for fun. But what about those behaviors and events that irk us? Why not take a moment every evening for a week or two to jot down what rubbed you the wrong way? Soon, you'll have a list that's basically a road map to better manage those feelings.

Here's a tiny secret: even the most self-aware folks have moments they don't see coming, those little blind spots that really shake their calm. How do you shine a light on those areas? You can do this through a team effort. Chatting with friends or seeking some professional advice can be a game changer. They offer fresh perspectives, helping you discover those hidden triggers.

Did you know that some cool science is helping us figure out stressors too? Researchers have found ways to spot stress in our bodies.[10] HRV is an incredibly important biometric indicator of stress. Your wearable gadgets keep an eye on it for you. When you see unusual peaks or valleys, try to match them with your day's events. Maybe you can find a pattern. Awareness is important, but what should you do once you're awake?

For the tech lovers, I created a tool called Pulse. This application is like a tiny stress detective for your life. It uses the latest stress-tracking science, pairs up with your wearable tech, and even syncs with your calendar to uncover those sneaky stressors. Plus, it's backed by years of expertise in managing workplace dynamics. The app even offers AI (artificial intelligence) coaching to give you tailored advice on navigating stress.

If you're aiming to truly thrive, keep an eye on those micro-stressors. They're not just pesky irritants but also a chance to grow and achieve more on your professional journey. Cheers to embracing them and soaring higher!

THIS IS YOUR BODY ON STRESS

That anxiety or tension we call *stress* makes it sound like it's all in your head, but it's in your body too. Mind and body are one. Stress will increase your heart rate and decrease your HRV. Stress increases blood pressure, tenses muscles, triggers excitement hormones, and cranks up your energy level, all in anticipation of the need for fight or flight. And the need for flight is in the mind of the beholder. It might be due to an enemy tank or an upcoming meeting with a negative coworker.

To understand what happens to your body under stress, consult some neuroscientists.[11] They'll tell you that the stress response engages the same brain-communication systems whether you're confronting a saber-toothed tiger or stuck in traffic. It calls up the forces of the voluntary and involuntary nervous systems, muscles, and metabolism, all to defend you from that perceived threat.

The somatic (voluntary) nervous system messages the muscles with a fight-or-flight response. The autonomic (involuntary) nervous system responds by sending nutrients and oxygen to the muscles. The sympathetic branch of the nervous system tells the adrenal medulla to release epinephrine (adrenaline), increasing the heart rate and relaxing the walls of your arteries so they accept that increased blood supply.

Meanwhile, the autonomic system's parasympathetic branch redirects blood flow away from your internal organs to increase flow to the muscles. Effectively, it slows down or stops your normal processes of digestion, tissue growth, organ maintenance, and kidney function so as to focus on activating the muscles. A cascade of stress hormones, such as cortisol, is pumped into the blood, releasing energy sources, such as sugar, into the system. They accelerate muscle function and perk up brain functions, including attention and learning.

That all sounds good, and this process readies the body and mind to combat the perceived stressor. But under chronic stress, the prolonged production of those stress hormones keeps your necessary normal functions, such as digestion and immune response, on the back burner. Your body is working so hard at fighting the stress response that it neglects its self-care. Prolonged exposure to those stress hormones affects brain functions, such as memory and reasoning. This accelerates aging and leads to sleep disorders, which in turn damage both physical and mental systems.

Now, you already know that what you expect to be stressful will be stressful. If you can't get relief over time, your body will burn out along with your mind. If you don't know how to deal effectively with what stresses you, you're out for the count. That's where resilience comes in. *Resilience is the ability to bounce back from stress, regain a healthy state, and go forward.*

> **If you can't get relief over time, your body will burn out along with your mind.**

NOT DEAD YET, BUT GETTING THERE

Back in 1888, German philosopher Friedrich Nietzsche stated, "Out of life's school of war—what doesn't kill me makes me stronger."[12] He was wrong. An extensive amount of research documents the disastrous impact excessive levels of stress have on employee performance.

Most studies of stress and employee performance suggest that as levels of stress increase, employee performance decreases. Studies have shown that excessive amounts of stress cause employees to be absent from work, quit their jobs, perform poorly at work, and suffer from physical ailments.[13] The negative effects of stress are not limited to the employee's work life.

Often, the stressors experienced at work will bleed over into other aspects of the employee's life. Work-stressed parents may be mentally and emotionally absent from family life, damaging the mental and emotional health of the whole family. Indeed, work stressors damage physical health and emotional health and drive counterproductive coping behaviors, such as drug and alcohol use and domestic violence.

Gallup's 2023 *State of the Global Workplace* reports not just increased stress among workers but also that 53 percent of workers say they want out and are looking for another job. Even more alarming, 44 percent of workers reported that they had felt a lot of stress the previous workday. Employee wellness, stress, mental health, and all the derivates of those terms have become top C-level initiatives recently, as this absolutely impacts the bottom line.[14]

Work offers benefits beyond the obvious financial incentives—purpose and the chance to focus on meaningful tasks. But it can be both rewarding and stressful at the same time. How do you deal with stress at work?

CASE STUDY: A COACH'S STORY

Mary was satisfied and felt that she was making a meaningful impact at her job as an executive coaching professional. She had great professional relationships and was well-known throughout the organization. But one day, while Mary was coaching her company's president on a presentation in front of other senior leaders, one of the newer vice presidents asked in an aggressive and condescending manner, "What's the main objective of this presentation?"

Unaccustomed to this tone, Mary was taken aback. She took a breath and looked at him, realizing this was not the time to address his attitude. She "kept calm and carried on" and continued through the end of the presentation. Following the meeting, she went straight to her office, where she was able to unpack the emotional stress of the previous hour.

Often, all it takes is one negative encounter to send our minds into a downward spiral of avoidance, rumination, anxiety, self-doubt, or other counterproductive states of mind. Even though Mary was working at the top of her game, this stressful interaction would have lingered in her mind over weeks or months, ultimately sapping her motivation and decreasing her overall performance. But it didn't.

Mary called on her internal resources and reexamined the validity of her coaching techniques and her relationship with senior management. She met with the executives and found common ground. She didn't let the stress fester in her coaching practice and work relationships.

STRESS IS MONEY

Unfortunately, as I talk with HR leaders, I find that investments in stress management, wellness, and mental health solutions are not seen as business drivers. They are pushed down deep in the HR organization and seen as an employee benefit or overhead. They're labeled as a cost of doing business. Most don't know the full gravity of the issue, the cost to organizations and their people, its root cause, and ultimately whose responsibility it is to deal with it. We are just now beginning to discuss these issues in the workplace, making them C-level initiatives in response to workforce needs, especially with Generation Z and millennials.

Here's one of the most startling numbers: *$300 billion is lost annually due to stress.* A review of research conducted in North America and Europe found that the financial cost of occupational stress was estimated to be up to $187 billion annually. But in 2019, the American Institute of Stress found that after including indirect factors, such as absenteeism, turnover, diminished productivity, increased medical costs, and increased legal costs, the total economic impact of stress to US employers was estimated at $300 billion.[15]

These real numbers are driven by missed days at work, lawsuits, breakdown in collaboration and innovation, turnover of key talent, and more. Can we really afford to see stress-reduction initiatives as just a cost of doing business?

Some other staggering statistics underscore the issue:

- 83 percent of workers experience stress at least once a week, with 16 percent reporting extreme stress.
- 81 percent of workers acknowledged that stress impacts their work negatively, manifesting in a range of symptoms from fatigue and anxiety to physical ailments and missed work.
- 50 percent of workers reported missing at least one day of work out of a year due to stress.
- 48 percent of all workers reported crying at work due to stress.[16]

According to Gallup's Negative Experience Index, which surveys working adults in 122 countries on the topics of worry, stress, sadness, and anger, 2021 broke records, and 2022 was on pace to surpass the previous year.[17] Many point to the pandemic as the driver; however, the uptick had started showing and growing back in 2015.

When stress won't quit and becomes chronic, workers burn out. Burnout is defined as the feelings of exhaustion, negativity, and ineffectiveness at work. The American Psychiatric Association Foundation's Center for Workplace Mental Health conveyed the daunting results of a 2020 Deloitte survey: 77 percent of professionals reported experiencing burnout at work. It's not just the white-collar workers who are feeling the heat. A 2020 Gallup survey found that 76 percent of all employees experience burnout. And a 2021 Catalyst survey found that 88 percent of workers felt burned out, with 60 percent in the severe range. That's a lot of toast in the workforce.[18]

As you have seen, *stressed employees affect the organizational bottom line*. Poor physical health and mental health cause workplace accidents, lost work time, and increased medical costs for the organization. Systemic organizational stress contributes to poorer work performance and lower quality of output (services and products). Stress breeds a cutthroat work environment, with employees avoiding the workplace or leaving their jobs altogether. The organization experiences a loss of productive workdays, a loss of key talent, and ultimately damage to profitability.

Examining the organizational consequences of stress, in the *Journal of Management*, researchers categorized the costs as direct and indirect costs.[19] Direct costs included absenteeism and turnover; performance on the job, such as accidents and poor-quality productivity; healthcare costs, such as insurance rates; and compensation payments, such as for sexual harassment. The indirect costs included loss of vitality, communication breakdowns, faulty decision-making, and quality of work relations.

In his presidential remarks to the American College of Occupational and Environmental Medicine, Edward Bernacki suggested that costs such as the following can be assigned financial value in morbidity and mortality:

- Direct costs of diagnosis and treatment of occupational and nonoccupational conditions
- Disability costs
- Higher wage costs
- Lost production
- Idle assets
- Employee turnover
- Planned overstaffing[20]

CASE STUDY: **IMPROVING COMMUNICATION AMONG NURSE LEADERS**

We partnered with a Tier 1 hospital that is a global leader in cancer research. Working with the staff, we found that creating a culture of safety where nurses can speak up and hold others accountable results in improved patient outcomes. We were honored the results were published in a peer-reviewed paper in the *Clinical Journal of Oncology Nursing.*[21]

Our project focused on refining the communication skills of nurse leaders and was designed to empower them with tools for deeper, more impactful conversations. The training had a statistically significant impact on improving communication skills and outcomes. It also proved that those conversations and skills do not exist in a bubble. We are all a part of a bigger culture and a culture of systems.

The nurse leaders were part of the hospital's Executive Nursing Council. They were experienced individuals, boasting master's or doctoral degrees and serving in leadership roles. Spanning seven modules, from Foundations to Confront, the program was tailored to address the various facets of communication.

Fierce Resilience offered nurse leaders the strategies to not only communicate better but also foster a sense of teamwork and accountability, essential for driving change. Yet this move is just one step. Going forward, changes need to be introduced at the organizational level. This will ensure accountability and cultivate a culture where quality and safety in patient care are paramount.

WORK STRESS IS THE WORST

The latest *Stress in America* survey in 2021 by the American Psychological Association revealed that more people said work was a source of stress compared to other sources, such as personal safety, housing costs, and personal health.[22] Stressors are linked to a large number of detrimental outcomes, such as depression, anxiety, burnout, intent to quit, decreased job performance, counterproductive behavior at work, and less job satisfaction.

Research has also shown that exposure to trauma increases our sensitivity to daily stress. In particular, those with PTSD are more likely to experience a heightened level of response to daily stressors. This increased sensitivity to stressors ends up intensifying PTSD symptoms, thus creating a spiraling stress-response cycle.[23] A lot of people in the workplace have experienced PTSD. We just don't know who they are.

Workplaces are just beginning to deal with the stress pandemic. The LinkedIn Learning *Workplace Learning Report* surveyed global leadership and development leaders on the most important skill sets for the workplace.[24] "Resilience and adaptability" ranked the topmost skill, while "dealing with stress" and "being more mindful" ranked eighth. Add the fourth-highest skill, "emotional intelligence," and you'll see the importance of Fierce Resilience.

Stress and performance are inextricably linked. As stress levels climb, performance declines, causing absenteeism, diminished work quality, and health issues. Stress takes a toll on mental and physical resources, making it harder to concentrate on tasks and leading to errors. Our organization, too, bears the

Take action to reduce stress in your workplace. You will save your life and that of your company.

financial weight of stress's burden, which gives rise to accidents, lowers our collective productivity, and even pushes valuable talent away.

Leaders must be particularly vigilant, monitoring both their own stress levels and those of their teams to maintain productivity.

And let's not forget that stress goes beyond the workplace; it seeps into our personal lives, affecting our families and even leading to harmful coping behaviors, such as substance abuse and domestic violence.

To overcome this challenge, *we need to face reality, acknowledge the effects of stress, and make stress management a cornerstone of our overall management strategy.* These stress-reduction techniques must go beyond the traditional ones. In the next chapter, I will take you through an explanation of what the term *resilience* has meant historically and how I am using it currently.

BUT IT'S NOT ALL BAD

I would like to leave you on a less stressful note—by highlighting the positive aspects of stress. While stress does lots of damage in the workplace and to the well-being of individuals, it does have benefits:

- Stress improves cognitive function by strengthening the connection between neurons in your brain, elevating memory and attention span, which equates to higher productivity.
- Stress helps protect your body from infections because moderate levels of stress produce interleukins, which gives your immune system a quick boost.
- Stress builds resilience. As you work through a tough situation, you begin to build muscle that allows you to better handle the next challenge.
- Stress motivates you to succeed. Think of the times you had a deadline for a project, an exam to study for, or a presentation to deliver. Stress stimulates the behaviors you need to manage those situations and get things done.

RESILIENCE REFRESHER

- Stress kills—literally.
- Workplace stress kills the organization, not just the individual.
- Stress-management training and its links to business results deserve C-level attention.

CHAPTER 3

EMPOWERING
SELF-AWARENESS

What I am looking for is not out there, it's in me.

—Helen Keller

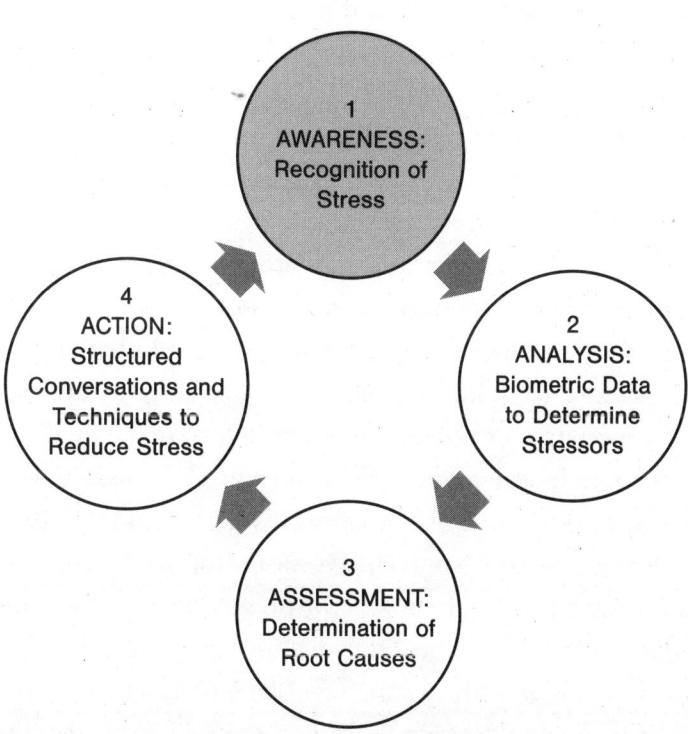

Figure 3.1. The Awareness Step

For twenty years, I was known as a finance expert and a numbers guy. However, my passion changed as my life and work experiences taught me the importance of resilience and managing stress. It all began during my first professional internship at a public accounting firm. The unfamiliar environment and culture made me feel stressed and pressured to think carefully before speaking, unlike how I was used to communicating.

One day, during an informal lunch with other interns and associates, I found myself in an uncomfortable situation. A woman with whom I also competed for top scores in college started boasting about her prominent lawyer family and successful CPA grandfather. Out of nowhere, she turned to me and asked about my grandparents in a snarky tone, putting me on the spot. In frustration, I defensively revealed that my grandparents were a bus mechanic and a domestic worker. I shut down the conversation after that, stewing in my anger and resentment. The internship ended on a sour note, at least in my mind.

Looking back, I realize that, like many people, I wasn't self-aware. In retrospect, I question my actions and contributions to the tense interaction. I should have approached the situation differently, taking a deep breath and providing private one-to-one feedback on how her remark made me feel.

If I had the chance to redo it, I would have initiated a conversation of feedback with her, clearing my context, assuming good intent, expressing my observations and feelings, and discussing how we could have worked collaboratively. This might have led to a friendship or a more positive working relationship that benefited both us and the company. Furthermore, the root issue was that I was insecure in how I spoke and presented myself in this culture that was foreign to me. These feelings were valid, but I should have shared them with my manager, HR representative, mentor, or coach instead of keeping them to myself. By doing so, I would have received support and guidance to overcome these challenges and create a more conducive work environment for myself and been able to focus on delivering my best work versus worrying about inconsequential issues.

This experience taught me the importance of self-awareness, constructive communication, and the decision to seek support when facing challenges. If I had the self-awareness to apply these lessons during my internship, the situation might have had a more positive outcome.

BECOMING SELF-AWARE OF EMOTIONS

The other important lesson that I have learned is how emotions dictate my response, leading to unnecessary hostility and stress. Emotions, deeply intertwined with physiology and cognitive processes, profoundly influence our thoughts, behaviors, and overall well-being. The ability to effectively navigate our emotional terrain is a testament to our cognitive sophistication and adaptability. While sometimes we think we leave our emotions at home, in truth, they are always present in the workplace.

When faced with emotional situations, these intricate emotional landscapes often shift abruptly, leaving you on uncertain ground with a profound effect on your thoughts, actions, and mental health that necessitates a constant balancing act. Yet amid this emotional turbulence, we reveal our resilience and capacity for growth, a testament to the intricate web of factors that constitute our humanity.

Emotional situations are a challenge, but they are also an opportunity to build resilience. A key strategy in dealing with stress is working with our own mental and emotional work of self-awareness and then reframing the stressful situation as more than just a roadblock.

A thought creates stressed feelings because we perceive that thought as threatening. We've told ourselves a story depicting the situation as dangerous and to be avoided. Then our behaviors grow from those stressed feelings. We avoid, dodge, sweat, and disengage. We become self-aware by asking ourselves these questions:

- What thought am I holding right now that is creating stress?
- What do I feel when I reflect on that thought?
- How do I behave when I believe that thought?

Then we can reframe our stories and thoughts and ask these questions:

- What do I feel when I reflect on that new thought?
- How can I behave when I believe the new thought?
- What can I do with this new insight?

This new way of looking at emotionally charged situations is transformational. Rather than running away with your old narrative of threat-danger-avoid, a Fierce Resilience mindset welcomes challenges with a new story of growth and strengthening. Follow these four steps to build your Fierce Resilience when negative thoughts start to take over:

1. *Stop*—Disrupt the negative thought cycle. Take a breath, go for a walk, and pick one activity to use as a trigger to pause every time you find yourself spiraling down into your old negative narrative.
2. *Reflect*—Reflect on the story you've told yourself. Lean into past experiences where you've overcome challenges. Are you overlooking important information?

3. *Recalibrate*—Tap into your inner resources, reassess, and adjust your approach. Shift the way you are thinking about something to one where you get better results.
4. *Choose*—Choose the path that best serves you. Which of these thoughts or stories will get you the best result?

In table 3.1, I have outlined questions to help you gain this self-awareness. As you see, I have borrowed from the hardiness model to frame them as Challenge, Control, and Commitment.

NAVIGATING EMOTIONS WITH CLIENTS

Building your self-awareness about emotions is a highly useful skill not only with yourself and coworkers but also with the life-blood of your business—your clients.

Evan was a real estate agent known for his impeccable professionalism and ability to close even the trickiest deals. One morning, he received a call that challenged his ability to navigate emotional situations. It was his elderly client, Rose, who had been his loyal client for many years. Her husband had recently passed away, and she faced the painful decision of selling their cherished family home.

Evan knew this was a pivotal moment for her. He understood that his role as a real estate agent had to evolve to include giving emotional support during this difficult time. He arranged to meet Rose at her home. As they sat in the cozy living room of the beautiful Victorian house, he could not help but notice all the memories of a life well lived and the tears welling up in Rose's eyes. He listened empathetically to her recount of stories about her late husband and the countless family gatherings they had hosted in that house.

Table 3.1. Achieving self-awareness and reframing your story

Challenge	Control	Commitment
Stop • What level of stress are you experiencing with it? **Reflect** • Why did you rate this level of stress that way? • What signs of stress are you noticing? • What stories have you told yourself about this? • How have you approached the situation in the past? **Recalibrate** • How else might you see this situation? • What positive aspects are possible in this situation? • How can you reframe your situation as a growth opportunity? **Choose** • What can you learn from this situation or experience?	**Stop** • How much control do you believe you have in this situation? **Reflect** • What aspects of the situation do you feel you can't change or influence? • Why or why not? **Recalibrate** • What part of the situation can you influence? • Where do you have control? **Choose** • As you consider where you do have influence, where would you start?	**Stop** • What's your level of commitment to resolving this situation? • How important is resolving this situation to you? **Reflect** • Why did you rate it that way? • What impact does it have on you and others? • What challenges do you foresee as you work through this situation? • How might you overcome them? **Recalibrate** • Who might you tap into for support? • Who might you invite into the conversation? • How might you deepen your level of commitment? **Choose** • How might you involve them? • What else will you do to ensure that you stay committed?

Source: Fierce Inc.

Feeling the weight of the situation, Evan realized he needed to act differently from his usual approach of discussing property values, market trends, and marketing strategies. He needed to help his client navigate the emotional aspect of selling her home while maintaining his professional responsibilities as an agent.

Evan began by acknowledging Rose's grief and validating her feelings. "I understand this is a difficult decision for you, and it's perfectly normal to feel this way. Your home holds so many precious memories, and it's natural to be attached to it," he said.

Rose, appreciating Evan's sensitivity, wiped away her tears and nodded. "It's just so hard. But I know I need to move on." She had clearly realized that this challenge was part of her life process, and she was committed to facing it.

Evan acknowledged his client's emotional reality. "I'm here to support you every step of the way. Let's work together to make this transition as smooth as possible. We can start by finding a buyer who will cherish this home as much as you and your late husband did."

Evan helped Rose focus on the future and the positive opportunities that awaited her. He said, "Think about what you want your next chapter to look like. Imagine a new place where you can create more beautiful memories and continue to honor your husband's legacy."

His client took a deep breath and envisioned a different future. "I suppose there are things I've always wanted to do but couldn't because of the house's upkeep," she admitted.

"That's right," Evan said with a warm smile. "Selling this house can be a step toward exploring those new passions." In this way, they worked together to reframe this emotional challenge as an opportunity for growth.

Over the following weeks, he continued to provide emotional support. He connected her with professionals to help with downsizing and moving. He encouraged her to document her cherished memories in a scrapbook, allowing her to hold on to the essence of her home.

As they worked together on marketing the house, Evan ensured his client was involved in the process, allowing her a sense of control. This involvement helped her reframe the sale as an opportunity to pass on her family's legacy to someone else who could create beautiful memories in the house. When they finally found the right buyer who appreciated the house's history and character, Evan made sure the transaction was handled with care and respect, providing a reassuring presence at the closing.

In the end, his client successfully sold her home and embarked on a new chapter in her life with a sense of resilience and strength she had never imagined. Evan's ability to navigate the emotional challenges of this situation, combined with his professional expertise, exemplified the principles of Fierce Resilience.

Both Evan and his client bounced not just *back* from this stressful situation but also forward: Evan bounced forward with a renewed confidence in his professional competence, grounded in emotional intelligence. Rose bounced forward into this next phase of her life, feeling emotionally validated and bearing a renewed sense of agency and control of her life path.

MOST OF US ARE UNAWARE

Unfortunately, many of us don't have the level of self-awareness that Evan did. Dr. Tasha Eurich, an organizational psychologist and executive coach, discovered that 95 percent of the five thousand workers studied in a five-year research project described themselves as self-aware. Yet only 10 to 15 percent really are.[1]

Overconfidence worsens as you go up the leadership ladder. Another study found that higher-level executives were less likely to accurately assess how their behavior affected those around them.

Experience and power create roadblocks to self-awareness. The more powerful we get, the less we reassess our ingrained perceptions and take feedback from peers.

Self-awareness is the key to identifying and dismantling the misperceptions and communication snafus that build up to break us down and burn us out. This introspection is an essential first step in busting stress and building Fierce Resilience.

Higher-level executives tend to be less likely to accurately assess how their behavior affects those around them.

INTERNAL VERSUS EXTERNAL SELF-AWARENESS

Dr. Eurich describes two types of self-awareness: Internal self-awareness is how clearly we see our own values, passions, aspirations, fit with our environment, reactions (including thoughts, feelings, behaviors, strengths, and weaknesses), and impact on others. Research shows that self-awareness results in higher satisfaction with jobs and relationships, better personal and social control, and happiness. Highly self-aware people are less likely to feel anxiety, stress, and depression.

External self-awareness, also known as social awareness, means understanding how other people view us, how clearly we know our social roles, and how well we are fulfilling them. Research shows that people who know how others see them are more skilled at showing empathy and taking others' perspectives.

When leaders' self-perceptions align with how their employees perceive them, they tend to have better relationships, feel more satisfied with them, and see them as more effective. But one type of self-awareness does not necessarily lead to the other: we can be high on internal self-awareness but blind to how badly we work with others.

INTERNAL AFFAIRS

If you have ever said about yourself, "I'm an introspective kind of person. I'm always critiquing and analyzing myself. How could I not know that I'm stressed out?" you are not alone.

Introspective people feeling stressed ask themselves, "Why do I do these things?" digging back into childhood traumas and perceived personality traits, but often come up with the wrong answers. They don't have conscious access to the deep, psychological reasons for their actions. They end up making up reasons for themselves and getting stuck in loops of negative rumination. If you're an Introspector on the self-awareness chart, you will likely be perennially unsatisfied with yourself and your job. As Susan Scott would say, "The stories we tell ourselves—not useful."

Rather than ask ourselves, "Why?" it's more effective to ask, "What?" Asking "What?" is practical and forward focused. It teaches you about your patterns of stressors and your behaviors in response to stress. It builds actionable internal self-awareness—for example, "I blew up at a coworker at that last staff meeting. What about that topic and situation is similar to others where I've blown up? What's causing this consistent feeling? What do those situations have in common? What's my pattern of stressful situations?"

CASE STUDY: CLUELESS TOO OFTEN

George grew up in a small town in Illinois. His family, with a history of entrepreneurship, instilled in him the value of self-promotion. He came from a long line of successful blusterers. George's gift for persuasion became evident when he was president of the Future Managers Club at Northwestern University. He later talked his way into being star salesman of the year in his first job at a midsize tech company. His ability to clinch deals and impress senior leadership led to a rapid ascent to management, and he was chosen to become CEO when the former leader stepped down.

His leadership led to an increase in profits but negatively affected the corporate culture. Employee morale was dropping. Innovation was stalling. Behind his back, George's overbearing communication style was pinpointed as the cause of discontent. He often dominated discussions, such as during the latest board meeting, where he had bombastically presented a five-year plan to a silenced table of board members. Behind closed doors, the board's concerns about him were growing. They had always appreciated George's strengths as a manager, but they began to see that he needed to be made aware of his suffocating effect on the people around him.

Ironically, George came out of his board meeting feeling great. "I killed it!" he thought. "Those board members ate up my proposal. Slam dunk, George!" But George hadn't seen the board members' eye rolls or their sighs of frustration as he spouted off for all but five minutes of the hour-long meeting. They couldn't get an idea in edgewise. Once George left the room, they discussed a possible out from his contract.

If you're externally self-aware, you know how your behavior affects others. You accurately understand how people see you and how you function in the group. You know your social roles and how well you're filling those roles. George suffered from what I would call *executive social blindness*. He was too full of his own power and too high up on the corporate ladder, isolated from reliable sources of feedback on how his behavior fit into the corporate social network. He was very low on the scale of external self-awareness.

Dr. Eurich and her team's survey of more than four hundred working adults in the United States found that 99 percent said they worked with a person like George—someone totally unaware of how his or her behavior affected others.[2] And their teams suffered: A clueless colleague cuts the team's chance of success in half. Coworkers are more likely to feel anxious and depressed and think of jumping ship. Working with people who are not self-aware ferments organizational stress and chips away at the bottom line. It feeds and amplifies toxic cultures.

A clueless colleague cuts the team's chance of success in half.

SELF-AWARENESS IS A STRESS BUSTER

To defuse stress, we need to identify the components of the stress process: the signs our body sends us that we're feeling stressed and the pattern of triggering situations where stress is generated for us. We can get these insights from internal and external self-awareness.

Some of the stress-management techniques I discuss in chapter 5 work on a platform of self-awareness—for example, mindfulness, for example. A University of Rochester study found that people who scored high on a measure of mindfulness also scored high on how well they accessed normally unconscious attitudes and emotional states.[3] In other words, these mindful folks were also more internally self-aware.

Certain jobs and situations generate high-stress levels, and self-awareness becomes a particularly powerful tool to get through a crisis. For example, in a natural or human-caused disaster, you face the danger of death, physical injury, or the loss of your home or even your community. You experience trauma that puts you at risk for mental, emotional, and physical health problems. Self-awareness is a powerful tool to get people through these times.

CASE STUDY: **BUILDING SELF-AWARENESS IN FIRST RESPONDERS**

Scott Winter is the CEO of Brain-Friendly Dynamics, where he uses his background in neuroscience and performance management to help individuals and teams thrive. One of his passions is building resilience in communities after natural disasters.

Scott lived near the deadliest and most destructive wildfire in California's history. The Camp Fire disaster in 2018 caused at least eighty-five fatalities, covered an area of 153,336 acres, and destroyed more than 18,000 structures. He remembers sitting in his home and feeling completely helpless. He became a search-and-rescue volunteer because he never wanted to feel like he couldn't go out and make a difference. He believes the number one cause of stress in our nervous system is feeling helpless.

Scott was asked to help develop resilience within the fire recovery space using his model of readiness, response, and recovery. Because a lot of people in the fire recovery space burn out, he focused on keeping them healthy, focused, calm, and alert. As part of his efforts, he worked at helping the first responders create self-awareness and to deeply tune in so they could cope. They needed to develop new muscles and take care of themselves to perform optimally. They needed to have feedback in terms of what their bodies were saying.

Scott says that during a crisis—whether a natural disaster or in business—people need to understand that struggling is part of the process. Often, we think something is wrong if we can't cope. The truth is that once we normalize and accept the struggle, we can move into recovery. To help people learn to struggle more effectively and recover more efficiently, the teams at Brain-Friendly Dynamics practice changing mindsets and using biofeedback tools to regulate stress after a traumatic event.

EMOTIONAL INTELLIGENCE: A CONTRIBUTOR
TO SELF-AWARENESS

The term *emotional intelligence* was coined in the nineties to describe a kind of smarts that had not yet received enough credit for facilitating human health and relationships. An emotionally intelligent person might be rotten at math but great at recognizing their own and other people's emotional or physical states. Both kinds of intelligence go a long way in the workplace. You need practical *and* emotional problem-solving skills. Emotional problem-solving lets people know when they're feeling stressed or when a coworker is about to go beyond their tipping point.

Emotional intelligence and its importance have been around for quite a while. It essentially instructs the value of acknowledging the emotion you are experiencing and building the muscle to be able to move to the logical side of your brain, process the issue at hand, and address it accordingly versus reacting purely on the emotion, which tells us we are vindicated because "you made me feel like this." This process, however, is distinct from true self-awareness.

As in the story of my first professional job, my feelings of being unseen, unheard, uncomfortable, intimidated, and offended were a common theme. And although I successfully managed my emotions, switched to my local intelligence, and won a highly competitive full-time position, I didn't understand why these feelings kept showing up. I would endure another ten years of agony and false narratives before my self-awareness identified a confidence issue that was quickly addressed once recognized. Then my personal and professional career flourished and continues to today.

This kind of smart person has a spy working on their side, gathering intelligence on the emotional (and the corresponding physical) responses to what's going on. They're a heart whisperer, able to pick up on and respond to emotions. Emotional intelligence gathering informs effective self-regulation and communication with others and builds self-awareness.

Sometimes, when we say, "I'm fine," we're not. Our heart rate is elevated, and maybe we start grinding our teeth, sweating buckets, or plotting early retirement. Physical and mental signs of stress often go unnoticed. Fear and anxiety work below the level of our conscious awareness. We know when we're stressed out only once it's too late.

Internal self-awareness is a mind-body activity. It's how we see our deep-seated values, attitudes, thoughts, behaviors, strengths, weaknesses, and stressors.

> **Our bodies bear the burden of stress.**

We've already learned from research that only 10 to 15 percent of us clearly understand ourselves according to self-awareness measures. That research didn't even consider a measure of our awareness (or lack thereof) of the stress-and-response process, working like an underground river below our level of consciousness. And that stress-and-response process is not just working in the depths of our psyches. Our bodies also bear the burden as stress hormones silently assault our heart rates, blood pressure, muscle tension, organ function, and brain function.

CASE STUDY: A HIGH PRICE

Linda, the COO of a prominent corporation, was known for their steady demeanor and sharp intellect. As someone who'd risen through the ranks, they were respected by peers and subordinates alike. Their upbringing instilled in them a strong work ethic. They grew up assisting in their father's grocery store, laying a foundation for their future in corporate leadership. They were considered tough but fair.

Despite their calm exterior, Linda was struggling to manage the dual pressures of a demanding job and a personal life without help from anyone. They were overseeing a major revamp of operations in the company's European plants, traveling almost nonstop, and assisting with the care of their mother, who was suffering from dementia. But if anyone had asked, they'd have told you they were doing fine.

Just after their fiftieth birthday, Linda suddenly passed away from cardiac arrest, leaving their colleagues in disbelief. How could someone so intelligent and effective at work be ignorant of what was happening inside them?

Many of us are like Linda: We are under a huge burden of stress but have trained ourselves to ignore the symptoms. We just forge ahead, building our careers and our companies on a foundation of confidence that holds strong—until it doesn't.

Linda was smart in business but lacked self-awareness and emotional intelligence, the ability to recognize, understand, and manage emotions. They were unwilling or unable to recognize their internal stress levels and psychological signs of stress. Their heart broke because it rarely got a break, beating at elevated levels to power their effectiveness but wearing itself out by spending too much time at that pace.

You can't live under constant stress. Linda was running at full speed too much of the time. They were at the low end of the emotional intelligence scale. It didn't have to be that way. If they had had a way to track what their heart was up to and reduced their stress, they might have saved their own life.

THIS IS YOUR BODY ON STRESS

For most people in most situations, the heart speeds up in response to stress. Elevated heart rate drains the body's resources faster. Too much time spent at an elevated rate can damage the heart, brain, and internal organs. Heart rate variability (HRV) has been found to be an indicator of cardiac health, psychological stress, and emotional regulation. Equally, HRV involves the interplay of several neurological systems, most notably the interaction between the sympathetic nervous system (SNS) and parasympathetic nervous system (PNS).

When under stress, the SNS increases our heart rate to provide much-needed blood and oxygen to our muscles to manage perceived threats. Once the threat is neutralized, our PNS lowers our heart rate, returning the body to routine organ maintenance tasks and conserving energy for the next challenge. However, if the SNS remains dominant, the heart rate remains elevated in response to continued perceived stress. The heart doesn't get the variation it needs over time. HRV remains in a too-narrow range, causing damage to the body and mind.

Fight and flight are two of our primal responses to threats. Humans need that shot of adrenaline to catch their prey or, more recently, project authority from our managerial persona. But the heart needs a break too. It must slow down sometimes and let the body shift its resources to mundane necessities, such as digestion, cell recovery, and restorative sleep.

Two branches of our nervous system coach the heart. The sympathetic branch riles us up to punch back when we see a challenge coming. The heart rate speeds up, gearing us to fight back. Then, when the challenger recedes, the parasympathetic branch is like the coach in our corner who fans us with a towel to calm us down between rounds. The parasympathetic system takes over, and the heart rate slows down.

In stress-fighting mode, the body sends its resources to the muscles for fight or flight. It heightens the senses to the threats of the outside world. It puts regular body-maintenance processes, such as digestion and tissue repair, on the back burner. In rest mode, the parasympathetic system tells the body to relax its external defenses and go back to the mundane but essential maintenance tasks of keeping the body going. Changes in heart rate go along with the shift between the heightened and relaxed states, speeding up in response to stress and slowing down when it's time to concentrate on the interior.

MEASURING STRESS WITH TECHNOLOGY

Since many of us, like Linda, are unaware of our stressed-out states, our bodies often pay the price before our minds even know we've been charged. What if we could use technology to identify the situations and relationships that cause stress? What if we could learn whether a stressed coworker is able to cool down and bounce back after stress? What if we could learn to be more self-aware of our own emotional states? What if we could augment emotional intelligence with a new kind of intelligence—biometric intelligence? HRV is an accurate measure of the stress response. Heart rate speeds up when you're stressed and slows down when you are not. It can be measured, and its changes can be tracked over time. A record of the changes in heart rate, from fast to slow and back again, is a record of the body's responses to stress and relief. HRV helps you understand what is stressing you out. This increased self-awareness, combined with action, will increase resilience.

What if you keep real-time track of your HRV, aligning its ups and downs with real-time events and situations? That would tell you when and how your body is responding to stress. Knowing this, you can build self-awareness. I'll

HRV is an accurate measure of stress response.

explain how you can get those metrics in the next chapter.

RESILIENCE REFRESHER

- Self-awareness is the foundation of stress-busting strategies.
- Though 95 percent of people believe that they're self-aware, only 10 to 15 percent actually are.
- Self-awareness can be taught, and traditional stress-management techniques help.
- You can reframe a stressful or emotional situation.
- HRV is a reliable metric of the body's response to stress.
- New tech solutions support self-awareness by tracking and analyzing HRV.

CHAPTER 4

USING BIOMETRIC INTELLIGENCE TO ANALYZE AND ASSESS ROOT CAUSES OF STRESS

I check my pulse, and if I can find it, I know I've got a chance.

—attributed to PAUL NEWMAN

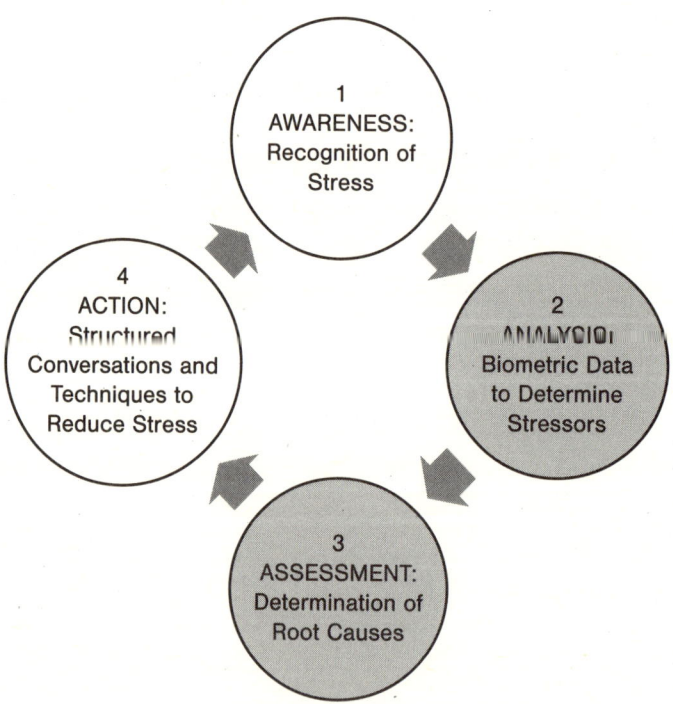

Figure 4.1. The Analysis and Assessment Steps

Anita, the regional head of sales for a division of a multibillion-dollar engineering services company, had a stellar ten-year record with rapid advancements. She was the first African American woman to hold her current position and, at age forty-five, was used to dealing with the race and gender microaggressions that were part of her everyday life, both on the job and off.

Her company had lost a major client, putting pressure on Anita and her team to replace the revenue. Unfortunately, two key salespeople were on medical disability leave, and HR's efforts to find suitable replacements were falling short. She needed to catch up on paperwork, and her team was still learning a new sales management enterprise system.

Moreover, recent policy changes from the executive team were not helping the overall collaborative company culture. They were slowing her access to the resources that had been critical to her success. On the personal front, she had just placed her mother in a nursing home, and her son was preparing for college. All of this was taking its toll on Anita as she navigated these challenges.

Anita would have described herself as a resilient and strong woman, but she was not feeling either quality. What she felt was overwhelming stress, but she couldn't quite pinpoint where the stress was coming from. All she knew was that she was exhausted, alienated, and disheartened. She never thought that stress was cumulative and that all stress was not alike. And she never knew there was a way to gather intelligence on stress in the same methodical way she had so deftly gathered intelligence on competitors.

NOT ALL STRESS IS ALIKE

Traumatic stress and everyday stress differ in their causes, intensity, and impact on an individual's well-being. Traumatic stress is a response to an extremely distressing or life-threatening event, such as natural disasters, accidents, violence, abuse, combat exposure, or the sudden loss of a loved one. In a work environment, it might be fear of losing a job, a significant job change, relocation, loss of a company, or what I continuously face, hitting our monthly, quarterly, and annual numbers. One recent example of traumatic stress for all of us was COVID-19, which impacted every aspect of our lives and made us live under constant fear for the health of ourselves and loved ones.

Everyday stress arises from the demands and pressures of daily life. Common triggers include work or school responsibilities, financial concerns, relationship issues, time management, and other routine challenges. Everyday stress is typically considered to be more manageable. It's often short-term and may dissipate once the stressful situation is resolved or the individual develops effective coping strategies.

Cumulative everyday stress, also known as aggregate stress, can have the same kind of mental and physical results as traumatic stress.

However—and it's a *big* however—cumulative everyday stress, also known as *aggregate stress*, can have the same kind of mental and physical results as traumatic stress: hypervigilance, emotional numbing, difficulty concentrating, and feelings of detachment from others. That's where Anita was heading.

THE DANCE OF AGGREGATE STRESS

Here's another analogy. Imagine yourself at a party, surrounded by all your friends and family. The music is lively, and everyone is dancing and having a great time. As you join the festivities, you notice the dance floor is getting increasingly crowded. People start stepping on each other's toes, and a few stumble and bump into others. It becomes clear that the more people join the dance, the more chaotic it becomes.

Let's relate this lively dance floor to the concept of aggregate stress. Just like with the crowded dance floor, our lives become a dance of multiple stressors intertwining with each other. If you come to understand the dance of aggregate stress, you become more adept at navigating personal and professional challenges without becoming overwhelmed. You need to be surgical to understand the root causes of issues that have culminated in your stressful life.

Like a skillful dancer, you can embrace the rhythm of life, managing stress with grace and resilience. Or you may be one of those people who will never get on a dance floor. Let's put aggregate stress in a business context:

- *The multitasking maze*—You're juggling multiple projects, answering emails, attending meetings, and trying to meet tight deadlines. Each task may be manageable, but when they pile up, you find yourself multitasking excessively. The constant switching between tasks leads to decreased productivity, increased errors, and heightened stress.
- *The challenging deadline dilemma*—You're part of a team working on a critical project with an approaching deadline. The pressure to deliver high-quality results within the given time frame is intense. Meanwhile, other deadlines and responsibilities are also lurking around the corner. The weight of meeting multiple demanding deadlines creates overwhelming stress, affecting your ability to focus and make sound decisions.
- *The communication cascade*—You work in a fast-paced environment where communication is essential. Constantly receiving emails, instant messages, and phone calls is stressful.

Moreover, if the communication is unclear or conflicting, it leads to confusion and added pressure to resolve misunderstandings promptly.

- *The role overload*—You have a specific job role, but additional responsibilities and tasks are gradually assigned to you over time. This role creep, or what consultants often refer to as *scope creep*, becomes burdensome as you find yourself stretched thin, trying to fulfill various roles without sufficient time and resources.
- *The team dynamics dance*—You work in a team with diverse personalities and work styles. While collaboration is essential, disagreements and conflicts among team members add to the stress. Managing team dynamics, particularly during challenging projects, is mentally and emotionally draining.
- *The performance expectations*—Your job requires you to meet high-performance standards consistently. While striving for excellence is commendable, an excessive focus on constant perfection creates an environment of chronic stress and fear of failure.

GETTING TO THE ROOT CAUSE

What if you had a way to gain awareness of the subconscious, physical workings of stress? This can be done through the use of biometrics: measuring biological states and processes. We can employ this twenty-first century tool to track our physical responses to our environment to gain self-awareness, adding another resource to our stress-busting toolbox.

In the previous chapter, I shared that research has found that HRV is a reliable measure of the stress response. The assessment involves not just taking your pulse occasionally but also mapping your HRV to your real-time surroundings and activities. You can then identify which situations stress you out (raise your heart rate and keep it elevated) and whether and when you eventually recover from stress (when your heart rate slows down). Let me share the past and current technology that gets you some answers to analyze the data and assess the root cause, as I have outlined in the Fierce Resilience Cycle.

A DRAMATIC CHANGE TO A
CENTURY-OLD APPROACH

The 1930s saw the introduction of the polygraph, a device designed to measure breathing rate, skin conductivity, blood pressure, and pulse. The rationale behind its application in criminal and security investigations was the belief that attempts at verbal deception would correlate with certain physiological responses. By the 1980s, technological advancements emerged that aimed to measure variations in speech patterns based on the same foundational theory. However, these approaches fell short when subjected to scientifically rigorous validity tests.

Exploring contemporary healthcare technology, especially biometrics, revealed an immense potential. This technology offered a valid and evidence-based feedback loop. For the first time, the typically invisible was made visible. Biometrics enabled individuals to monitor their physiological stress levels and utilize this information. The technology fostered a systemic connection between an individual's physiological state and intentional, conscious actions to alleviate stress.

Now, add in the psychological dimension of artificial intelligence (AI). A wearable device could easily warn us of impending emotional outbursts, given that the physical signs were not challenging to detect. Emotions, often lurking beneath the surface, occasionally bubbled up in moments of intensity. An AI tool with timely intervention capabilities is invaluable, especially when recognizing the delicate threshold before emotions become consciously palpable. By identifying these early biological pre-conscious indicators, we can proactively prevent emotional esca-lations and analyze and understand triggers in real time to drive self-awareness and learning.

The combination of wearable sensors, a historical database, and finely tuned algorithms has paved the way for heightened self-awareness, which is the initial step toward making conscious behavioral choices. *Essentially, biometric feedback refers to using physiological measurements to monitor the body's responses to stressors.* By leveraging biometric data, individuals and leaders gain valuable insights into the impact of stress on physical and mental well-being. I call it *biometric intelligence.*

It allows us to align heart rate changes with a record of work-place activity. If a work task or a workplace conversation cranks up the heart rate meter, that person is experiencing stress. It doesn't matter whether an outsider thinks that situation should be stress-ful. Stress is in the heart of the perceiver of stress and is different for each person.

When the heart rate starts to slow down after a peak, the individual either perceives that the stressor is diminishing or is applying emotional self-regulation skills, even when the stressor persists. Or their heart rate might stay up, depriving the individual of needed respite from stress. They then continue in the stressed state, unable to control either the emotion or the source of stress to bring the heart rate down.

Research has found that mindfulness training and cognitive reappraisal teach us to regulate emotions and, therefore, our reac-tions to perceived stress.[1] By regulating emotions, we increase HRV, building a healthy balance between elevated and reduced stress levels. Biometrics give us an awareness of the emotions we need to regulate.

BENEFITS OF BIOMETRIC INTELLIGENCE

Leveraging biometric intelligence has amazed leaders and employees, who have used it with the benefits seen in table 4.1.

Table 4.1. Ten ways to benefit from biometric intelligence

Benefits	How we benefit
1. Self-awareness	Provides individuals real-time data on people's physiological responses to stress. Helps raise awareness about the body's reactions to various stressors, allowing individuals to identify patterns and triggers contributing to aggregate stress.
2. Stress identification	Detects signs of stress even before individuals consciously recognize them. By identifying stress early on, individuals take proactive steps to mitigate its impact and prevent it from accumulating into aggregate stress.
3. Biofeedback techniques	Helps individuals learn to control their physiological responses, such as heart rate and breathing. By mastering these techniques, individuals better manage stress in real-life situations.
4. Personalized stress management	Allows for personalized stress-management plans. Each individual's stress response is unique, and biometric data helps tailor stress-reduction strategies based on their specific physiological patterns.

continued

Table 4.1. Continued

Benefits	How we benefit
5. **Real-time feedback**	Monitors aggregate data on stress levels within teams. For example, wearable devices provide real-time data on stress responses during critical projects or high-pressure periods.
6. **Objective assessment**	Offers an objective measure of stress levels, reducing the reliance on subjective self-assessment, which is especially helpful in situations where individuals may underestimate or overlook their stress levels.
7. **Long-term progress tracking**	Allows individuals to track their stress-management progress. By analyzing trends in the data, individuals identify the effectiveness of their stress-reduction strategies.
8. **Biofeedback-assisted relaxation**	Facilitates relaxation techniques. For instance, individuals engage in guided meditation or breathing exercises while monitoring their biometric data to reduce stress effectively.
9. **Health and wellness programs**	Offers an opportunity to incorporate biometric feedback into workplace wellness programs. Providing employees with biometric devices and stress-management resources promotes a culture of well-being.
10. **Early intervention**	Enables early detection of chronic stress, allowing for timely intervention and support. Addressing stress early prevents it from escalating into more severe mental or physical health issues.

Source: Fierce Inc.

SHOULD YOU BE SKEPTICAL?

Biometric feedback is a relatively new field with room for lots more research. The studies that have been done, however, are quite promising. By learning to self-regulate their HRV through relaxation techniques, participants reported experiencing improved mental and emotional well-being. In the workplace context, some studies have explored the impact of HRV biofeedback on employee stress levels. Findings suggest that employees who received biofeedback training experienced reduced stress and improved overall well-being.[2]

HRV biofeedback has been associated with increased resilience to stress. Participants who received biofeedback training demonstrated greater adaptability and coping skills in challenging situations. Learning to control HRV through biofeedback exercises also enhances self-regulation abilities. Participants better managed their physiological stress responses and could shift their bodies into a more relaxed state when needed.

HOW I GOT IMMERSED IN BIOMETRIC INTELLIGENCE

I'm a data nerd who loves numbers and measurement, as is Gabe, my chief behavioral science officer at Fierce. We share a passion for reducing stress and building resilience in the workplace to help individuals and organizations reach their desired results.

Gabe has always loved data and finding out what makes people tick. That's why he went into industrial psychology and spent ten years with the Naval Center for Combat and Operational Stress Control. When we started working together, his research savvy and data skills helped confirm the statistical linkages between the application of Fierce Conversations and lower stress, higher resilience, and goal attainment. Gabe's data analysis showed that improved interaction skills tracked along with stress reduction. Communication skills enable the engagement with others that is necessary for resolving stressful relationships and scenarios. And any successful engagement is based on self-awareness.

I am a prime example. When I started my career, I noticed that I was often dealing with feelings of intimidation and being threatened in my work environment. I had learned to manage my emotions well, which helped me succeed. However, later in my life, as I was transitioning into leadership roles, I ran into issues with how I saw myself and reacted to others. I began practicing emotional intelligence, but it didn't address the root causes of these issues. While counseling, I learned about some deep-rooted insecurity issues that had begun when I was a child.

But not everyone makes the choice to seek counseling or has the means, particularly when they are living a generally successful life at work and home. I wanted to help others like me who were letting stress get in the way of their happiness. I was also compelled by my personal interest in sports performance.

As an avid road cyclist who constantly analyzed my heart rate to optimize my performance, I saw the potential for applying the same concept to workplace stress and performance. Heart rate data provides insights into stress levels and helps individuals manage their responses effectively. My experience as an athlete and the use of wearable devices played an important role in connecting the dots.

DEVELOPING THE FIERCE APP

I led the team at Fierce to create an app that offered step-by-step guidance for real-world situations, making it easy for people to navigate conversations and interactions—a Fierce Conversations wizard in your pocket when you needed it. Like many organizations, as we embarked on a digital transformation, we recognized the importance of making learning sustainable in leadership training. Traditional leadership-development companies followed a linear approach, offering workshops and training sessions for specific skills, but then left learners to remember and apply the concepts later, often with limited success. The learning was not sustained.

Additionally, millennials and Gen Z desired a more practical and relevant approach where learning was integrated into their day-to-day work experiences, so we set out to design a solution that would provide real-time, on-the-spot guidance and support rather than expecting learners to recall concepts from weeks-old training materials. Through direct collaboration with end learners, we developed Fierce Connect. This app included an analytic wizard that determined the appropriate conversation technique for the situation. It then offered step-by-step guidance on approaching and delivering critical conversations along with additional resources, such as blog posts, Q&As, and a coach's corner.

The response from our customers was positive, but they were not using it at the levels we would have anticipated. I talked with people in the workplace and found that in the moment of contentious interactions, worry, or other scenarios, they weren't thinking, "Let me grab my phone in my pocket to find a solution." It made sense given that the physical state they were in was stressed. A lightbulb went off.

I started to learn about connected strategy and realized we could use technology to help people in their moments of stress. A connected strategy is a business model that harnesses the power of technology and data to create seamless connections within a company and with its customers, partners, and stakeholders.

I was particularly struck by the customer-centricity of the model, with its strong focus on understanding and meeting people's needs through data-driven insights and personalized interactions at every point of contact. Also appealing was the idea of real-time decision-making utilizing data analytics, wearable devices that track heart rate in real-time, and artificial intelligence. This would allow development of algorithms to promote an assessment of root causes and subsequent actions to make it easy for people to turn their insights into actions. *We essentially are able to be there when people need us by reading how they were experiencing their environment.* The result was Pulse, a biometric intelligence tool that works in sync with the human experience. I am proud to be the innovator and patent inventor of Pulse.

AI bots and in-person coaches provide targeted stress-busting strategies based on data.

By being linked to a live coach or AI bot, Pulse drives self-awareness and leads people to tackling their stressors, increasing their resilience and progressing them toward their personal and professional goals. For example, if biometric intelligence helps a person determine that a key cause of their stress is a difficult relationship with a colleague, the bot, Susan (yes, I named it after Susan Scott, who is the ultimate guide), would recommend preparing for and carrying out a difficult conversation with that colleague. A quick tutorial educates the individual and provides exercises to prepare them for that conversation. Pulse then looks for reduced stress metrics after that conversation resolves the source of stress. Then it moves on to the next stressor.

Data privacy remained paramount, so we made sure that individual data is shared only with the person and their chosen coaches. However, we are providing aggregate and anonymous resilience data to help companies identify stress hot spots and intervene before issues escalate, benefiting the company and its workforce.

CASE STUDY: BUILDING SELF-AWARENESS OF THE ROLE OF ALCOHOL ON STRESS

Don, a thirty-five-year-old man, believed that drinking a few beers after a long day or week helped him to relax. However, he began to notice that his anxiety and stress levels were amplified the day after consuming alcohol.

Stress data analysis showed that his HRV significantly dropped during days and nights of consuming alcohol. The heart rate stayed at its elevated rate with little variation. This reduction in HRV indicated increased stress events both during sleep and the following day. Normal routine challenges drove more irritability and lowered his willingness to solve problems. The effects of alcohol show up as reduced HRV even during sleep.

With this newfound understanding, Don became more conscious of when and how much alcohol he could drink, considering its impact on his resilience. For instance, when facing high-stakes meetings or critical interactions the next day, he made the informed decision not to consume alcohol. He also learned to recognize situations, such as children's events or family gatherings, where alcohol consumption might be better avoided. This biometrically generated knowledge became a cornerstone of his resilience going forward.

As a result of these mindful decisions, Don reported a 10 percent increase in overall HRV and an improved ability to focus and maintain self-awareness during critical events. The case highlights the importance of understanding individual triggers and making conscious choices to manage stress effectively, offering him a critical Fierce Conversation with himself!

BIOMETRIC DATA TRACKING IS WORKING

Data compiled from people using Pulse shows a 10 to 15 percent reduction in stress, although 30 to 50 percent is typical; an 8 percent reduction in burnout; and a 14 percent reduction in anxiety. We are seeing an 11 percent increase in resilience, a 4 percent increase in team cohesion, and a 4 percent increase in organizational commitment. These results are attained after two weeks of using Pulse plus one ninety-minute coaching session or AI bot intervention.

Research backs up our experience. *An independent study by Mount Sinai Medical Center validated the potential of wearable devices like Pulse for measuring well-being and resilience.*[3]

This further reinforced my belief that biometric intelligence guides targeted action and constructive conversations. Here are some of the benefits we are observing:

- Lowers stress in the workplace so employees thrive, who then go on to drive measurable results to the bottom line
- Shows differences in populations across important demographically focused initiatives, such as diversity, equity, and inclusion and remote, in-person, and hybrid workplaces
- Helps corporate cultures provide feedback, psychological safety, and clear lines of direction and communication, and eradicates workplace toxicity
- Aggregates data to enable organizations to measure and build resilience from a predictive versus lagging perspective.
- Provides data that show patterns of stress within an organization

For coaches, Pulse became a game-changer by uncovering insights that transformed coaching sessions from subjective conversations to deep analyses based on factual data. Coaches could use that data to show patterns in a stress response that had been below a level of consciousness, leading to greater self-awareness and personal growth. Empowered with insights from Pulse biometric data on an individual's stressors, a coach walks into a coaching session ready to help the individual attack those stressors directly. They can plan the needed conversations and plot changes that address stress at its source.

We are seeing profound, immediate results from just one ninety-minute coaching session. Why is this happening? The core reason is that coaches get accurate data unavailable using traditional coaching methods. Traditional coaching takes multiple sessions before the counselor gets down to what might be the real issue. Even then, it's based on the perception of the problem by the person being coached. With biometrics, the coach can see actual data about what the person is reacting to and help them understand what's happening at the moment of stress. They immediately see it, and the coach can move them into self-awareness to get results. Quite simply, we've truncated the time and process of traditional coaching methods and can tie the data back to business results.

Biometric intelligence allows us to analyze stressors and assess root causes of stress, unlocking self-awareness to greater levels. That leads to action in the form of traditional stress-management techniques, structured conversations, and other relevant interventions. Let's move forward into the next chapter to discuss some traditional management techniques.

RESILIENCE REFRESHER

- Traumatic stress, everyday stress, aggregate stress—the body feels them all, but the mind is not always aware.
- Biometrics are measures of the body's response to stress.
- Biometric intelligence from measures such as HRV provides insider information on what's happening inside the body under stress.
- Biometric intelligence is enhanced self-awareness and the foundation of emotional intelligence.
- Biometric data helps pinpoint stressful situations.
- Coaches and individuals, once aware of sources of stress, can target stress-busting solutions.
- Pulse measures and aggregates HRV data, analyzing individual and organizational patterns of stress.
- Linked to AI, live coaching, and data banks of stress-busting solutions, Pulse users have shown reduced stress in record time.

CHAPTER 5

TRADITIONAL APPROACHES TO STRESS MANAGEMENT

Remind yourself. Nobody built like you, you design yourself.

—Jay-Z, "A Dream"

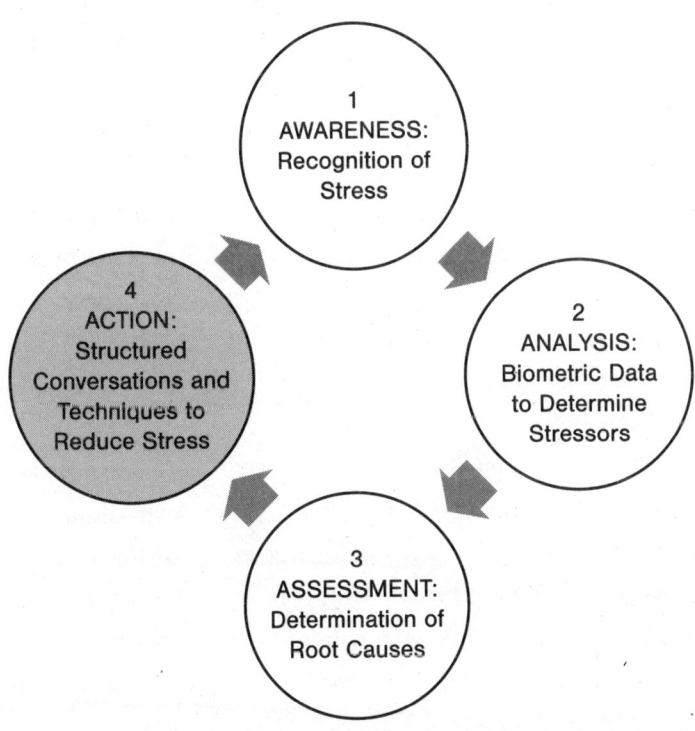

Figure 5.1. The Action Step

You have seen that stress kills, and even when it doesn't kill, it damages the body and slashes performance. Humans have been battling stress since we faced our first saber-toothed tiger. We've had a lot of time to get it right, so how are we doing at the stress-busting game?

Mindfulness, meditation, and communication training are a trio of tools that help us reduce stress both professionally and personally. Mindfulness is a form of meditation during which we try to be fully present in the moment without judgment. It asks us to focus on the current sensations in the body, allowing judgmental thoughts to simply move through and out of the mind. An exercise in mindful eating, for example, might have you fully experience eating a single raisin, focusing your awareness on its taste, its texture, and the feelings in your mouth and throat as you chew and swallow. Nothing else matters in that moment other than that raisin. With repeated practice, mindfulness meditation has been shown to reduce our anxiety and perception of stress. Mindfulness is to live in the present, not wrapped up in the mind's never-ending judgments, fears, and assumptions.

Picture the following scenario. You're at work, feeling overwhelmed by the tasks piling up and the looming deadlines. Mindfulness training would have you pause, focus on the here and now, and let the downward-spiraling fear of failure float through you and away. Stress starts in the mind, and mindfulness teaches you to simply let it go.

Mindfulness practices also encourage you to engage your attention to focus on sensory stimuli. When you concentrate on breathing and bodily sensations during meditation, the analytical part of your mind can't help but start to evaluate these sensations. But mindfulness interacts with other attention networks to nudge your mind back to the experience of the present sensation and away from judgmental thoughts and perseverative worries. Studies show that long-term practitioners of mindfulness change the activity and structure of their attention networks.[1] You learn to live in the moment.

Repeated practice of mindfulness strengthens the ability to stay in the present and ignore distractions and anxiety-producing thoughts. Neuroscience shows that it makes real changes in the brain.[2] It builds executive control over the activation of attentional networks that are normally outside of our awareness. Mindfulness practice is like going to the gym and doing heavy chest presses and arm curls but for our mind. Our stress-busting skills get stronger, including our self-awareness.

Leaders at work will especially benefit from this skill. When leaders practice mindfulness, their employees notice a positive change. They feel treated more fairly, experience less stress, and perform better overall.

Traditional stress-management tools like meditation are all about detaching from the mind's constant chatter of judgment and speculation. It's like a mental workout. Some types of meditation have us focus on an image or phrase or simply empty our minds of words and images. Guided meditations transport us to serene places, such as a peaceful forest or a beautiful beach, to calm our minds and reduce our stress.

Companies that have offered meditation training to their employees find that emotional intelligence gets a boost, perceived stress goes down, and feelings of depression and burnout diminish. Job satisfaction and performance see an improvement too. Mindfulness and meditation training is a foundation of employee development in many Fortune 500 companies: Apple, Google, General Mills, Goldman Sachs, and Nike. At Aetna, mindfulness training contributed to a $6.3 million savings in employee healthcare costs.[3]

PRACTICE, PRACTICE, PRACTICE:
HOW ELITE ATHLETES DEAL WITH STRESS

When an athlete's mind is overflowing with anxiety from fear of failure, the mind and the body choke. Some people call it "paralysis by analysis" or simply overthinking. Elite athletes have thus found ways to flush the mind, focus on the moment, and go with the flow.

It all comes down to mind over matter. So much research into psychological skills training for athletes has been published that it warranted a bibliographic analysis in 2023. Researchers found four categories of psychological training: (1) stress, mental toughness, and coping; (2) management of anxiety, motivation, self-confidence, and self-efficacy; (3) training in flow and mindfulness; and (4) management of emotions.[4]

Researchers from Loughborough University reviewed stress-management interventions with sports performers, organizing their work according to the ways that interventions attack stress.[5] An intervention aims to do the following:

- Reduce the stressors
- Modify the athlete's cognitive appraisal of the situation
- Reduce negative emotions and increase the positive
- Facilitate effective coping behaviors

LeBron James meditates, as do Serena Williams, Michael Jordan, and Tom Brady. Championship golfer Annika Sörenstam never had a bad shot: she analyzes her mistakes and then forgets them. Elite athletes have been practicing stress management forever, and they're a great source of wisdom on how the mind and body are one. They know that peak physical performance must be grounded in mental and emotional preparation. Before they blast into action, they have practiced being still.

LeBron can be seen meditating right there on the bench. He explained, "Meditating helps a lot for me personally with taking a lot of deep breaths, closing my eyes and just centering myself and listening to my inner self . . . That definitely is something that keeps me sane in the bubble."[6]

LeBron is in the game; he is the leader and a major contributor to his team's success. He doesn't have the luxury of going home, grabbing his beverage of choice, and going to bed. The game is on the line. This parallel is similar for us in the workplace. Every moment and every interaction counts.

Serena practiced silent meditation when she was competing, using the "just observe" response when thoughts crossed her mind. Let it go, let it go! She wasn't frozen by distractions but instead simply let them go, repeatedly returning to that quiet place at her center. Then, she went out and slammed that one hundred miles per hour serve into center court.

Michael had great coaches with the Bulls and the Wizards, but his most important trainer was his mindfulness meditation coach. His meditation practice started with focusing on becoming fully aware of everything around him by noticing, observing, and reserving judgment. Then, he let go of it all and focused on his breath in the present moment. Mindfulness often has you focus on the breath as it comes in and goes out, letting thoughts pass through the mind unjudged and unanalyzed.

What does mindfulness meditation do for these elite athletes? It teaches them self-regulation, including attention control, emotion regulation, and self-awareness. When the game gets crazy out there—when LeBron gets that three-pointer from center court—they're grounded in those earlier moments when they sat quietly, alone, feeling the breath go in and out, thinking of nothing.

ATHLETES AND GRATITUDE

Athletes have another trick up their sleeve—practicing gratitude to improve their sports performance. They know that staying healthy is sometimes beyond their control. Physical setbacks happen every day to both professional and amateur athletes, so the ability to move your body is something to be grateful for. It creates appreciation of what you can do in the moment and improves resilience.

Counting our blessings with gratitude brings a plethora of goodness into our lives. Focusing on the sunnier side keeps those gloomy feelings of anxiety,

Gratitude is a resilience booster.

depression, and stress at bay. Plus, sprinkling gratitude into our interactions makes our bonds with others stronger and warmer. And guess what? Scientific research proves that gratitude not only brightens our mood but also gifts us better sleep and a stronger immune shield.

Gratitude is a resilience booster. Keeping our spirits high, even when the chips are down, becomes a tad easier. It gives us these cool glasses to see hurdles as stepping stones, teaching us and helping us grow. By celebrating the good around us, we are prepped to face challenges with a smile and keep our emotional sails steady amid life's storms.

Let's chat about the magic of gratitude and resilience in our workspaces. Did you know that sprinkling a little gratitude in our daily work interactions not only spices up our personal lives but also adds a zesty flair to our office vibes? By sharing a simple "thank you" with our teammates and leaders, we're actually laying bricks for stronger bonds and a happier workspace.

Picture this: A sales team is hustling hard but still falling a bit short on their targets. Instead of letting disappointment reign or letting a cutthroat competition vibe seep in, the savvy team leader shifts gears. They rally the troops to celebrate the good stuff, such as the awesome rapport they've built with clients or the satisfaction of helping customers find just what they need. With this gratitude pep talk, a fresh wave of enthusiasm and drive fills the air.

Let's not forget the magic of the *witnessing effect*. Ever heard of it? Kudos to the brilliant Sara Algoe from the world of psychology and neuroscience for this gem.[7] Here's the deal: When you openly show gratitude to a colleague, it's like casting a little spell. Everyone who sees this act starts seeing the one you thanked in a new, radiant light. It's almost like they've got this invisible "Super Helper" badge on! This gratitude show-and-tell transforms team dynamics in the most fantastic way.

TAKE THE BALL AND RUN WITH IT!

Elite athletes take time-outs for stress management because their coaches see how it improves their game, and a better game makes more money. Their investment in stress management ups their stats. But what about *our* stats?

Now that you know that workplace stress costs our businesses $300 billion per year, isn't it time to bring the wisdom of the playing field into our staff rooms and executive suites? Learn to manage stress like those elite athletes and power up your performances. Let's win those championships as a team.

THE THRILL OF SKIING AND MANAGING STRESS

Have you ever been downhill skiing? Remember that exhilarating feeling from the first time? As you stood on top of the hill with skis on, anxiety and stress probably engulfed you. The cold air swirled around you, yet you felt sweat trickling down your face and back. You may have been experiencing an inner battle or giving yourself a mental pep talk before you took that leap downhill. Those first few moments were probably filled with fear, especially the fear of falling. But as time passed and with more practice, those stress reactions didn't just vanish. They evolved and transformed.

Seasoned skiers often talk about that same initial rush. But for them, they feel a blend of exhilaration and joy. What changed over time? Your experiences turned those initial stressors into driving energy, converting stress into a source of heightened performance.

Back in the early twentieth century, when Hans Selye first started talking about stress, it primarily referred to distressing situations causing both emotional and biological reactions. However, as he delved deeper, he realized that similar reactions also were triggered by positive events. This led him to coin the term *eustress* to differentiate between negative and positive stressors.[8] The combining form *eu-* comes from the Greek for "good."

Eustress = peak performance

While our stress response is fundamentally a survival mechanism, alerting and preparing us for potentially harmful situations, its effects aren't always beneficial. The real challenge arises when stress becomes a chronic presence in our lives, keeping us in a perpetual state of heightened alertness. Over time, this leads to serious health issues, including anxiety, burnout, and depression.

In the short term, stress amplifies our decision-making and problem-solving abilities, especially when we're immediately confronted with a stressful scenario. However, prolonged stress deteriorates these skills, impacting our overall well-being and efficiency.

HOW TO FOSTER A RESILIENCE NETWORK

Boosting resilience against stress isn't just about individual tactics. Engaging in friendly conversations, teaming up, offering feedback, and mentoring solidifies trust and creates a safe space among your peers. Cultivate nurturing relationships that amplify resilience.

Think back to ancient times. Families and clans built strong connections to defend against various challenges. Over time, these bonds gave rise to protective structures, such as community walls. Fast-forward to today. While you may not always visibly identify threats, you grapple with unseen pressures in your daily life. Imagine your network as a protective shield against life's stressors. By nurturing healthy relationships, you not only protect yourself but also harness the collective resilience, making daily challenges easier to tackle.

Here's a captivating story from medical history that underscores the might of community support. In the early 1960s, researchers keen on combatting cardiovascular disease began observing communities with notably good health. Surprisingly, they found a community in Pennsylvania where folks didn't exactly follow the healthiest lifestyles. Despite their dietary choices and habits, this community outshined others in terms of health and joy.

The secret? The people felt a deep sense of community. Originally an immigrant settlement, this area stood out because of its tight-knit bonds and traditions. The collective strength of the community seemed to cast a protective aura of resilience around its members.[9]

Think about your own journey. I recall a time early in my career that beautifully showcased the strength of a resilient network. Working in a competitive sales domain was no cakewalk. Despite facing numerous challenges, I flourished thanks to the unwavering

> **Imagine your network as a protective shield against life's stressors.**

support of my colleagues. We'd chat daily, have each other's backs, travel together, and even enjoy off-hours as a close-knit group.

Their support was the anchor that kept me grounded and optimistic. Table 5.1 offers six suggestions to build a resilience network.

Always remember, building resilience is like cultivating a garden: it takes time, love, and patience. But with a robust network of relationships, you're not just planting flowers, you're crafting a sanctuary. Engage in heartfelt conversations, be an active listener, and cocreate a nurturing environment. This journey requires effort, but the blossoms of trust, support, and resilience are worth every step.

A FAILURE TO COMMUNICATE

In the first chapter of this book, I talked about the four Cs and discussed the importance of adding the fifth C—conversations—to the list. Some leadership-training programs address stress management through communication training. In our own research, we found that 90 percent of communication issues arise from misunderstandings, a simple lack of clarity, or a lack of awareness of the impact our behavior has on others. Poor communication produces stressful relationships and avoidable circumstances.

Communication training helps us be more confident and effective in our interactions. Imagine being able to connect, support, and influence people both at work and in our personal lives with ease. Communication-skills training boosts confidence and leaves consumers and clients more satisfied.

Many communication-skills training programs are aimed one way, however, teaching managers how to better communicate to employees. They fail to acknowledge that communication means interaction: it's a two-way street. They also leave out the prep work that's essential to a successful interaction. We need to dig deep and do the groundwork behind that interaction. What are the interpersonal misunderstandings that have made this interaction

Table 5.1. Six ways to build a resilience network

Steps	Description
1. Nurture your inner circle.	Find those special folks in your life you lean on and share secrets with. These may be your buddies, coworkers, team leaders, or even life mentors.
2. Strengthen heartfelt bonds.	Cherish moments with these dear ones. Whether you're grabbing a cozy coffee, breaking a sweat together at the gym, or just exchanging fun tales and memories, make each moment count.
3. Chat with an open heart.	Embrace openhearted conversations with your circle. Let them into your world, express your feelings, and lend an ear when they open up. Mutual trust and understanding are golden.
4. Seek a helping hand.	Whenever life feels overwhelming, don't hesitate to tap into your support system. Pinpoint areas where you feel a little shaky, find someone who excels there, and soak up their wisdom. Whether you're facing a storm or just crave a heart-to-heart moment, remember your circle has your back.
5. Spread the love.	Take a moment every now and then to shower your network with appreciation. A simple thank you or gesture makes a world of difference.
6. Embrace and celebrate diversity.	Broaden your horizons by connecting with a diverse group. Different strengths, backgrounds, and perspectives enrich our lives and offer unique solutions to challenges.

Source: Fierce Inc.

necessary? How do employees see the problem? How has it affected them? What is our own role in it? Successful communication training has to teach human problem-solving as well as presentation skills.

BEYOND TRADITIONAL STRESS MANAGEMENT TO FIERCE RESILIENCE

Corporate trainers know the cost of stress on the employee and the organization's bottom line, and they know something can be done. Resilience can be taught, and corporate training has had great results. This is what I know from years of working with individuals and training organizations:

- Stress is killing us, but many of us can't identify exactly what's stressing us out.
- Self-awareness is essential to stress-busting. You need to know your own personal stress demons as well as how your behavior affects others.
- You can pinpoint those stressor demons if you attend to what the body's up to and leverage twenty-first-century biometrics.
- The stress is often generated from human-interaction issues. Effective stress-busting requires sitting down with those humans and working things out through conversation.
- No ordinary conversation will do the job. You need to know how to have Fierce Conversations and peel back the layers of miscommunication and misunderstanding, dismantling the stressor at its source.

RESILIENCE REFRESHER

- Traditional stress management uses meditation (including mindfulness training) and communication-skills training.
- Elite athletes use these techniques to up their game.
- Companies that provide stress management training have seen financial benefits.
- Those traditional techniques have been helpful, but the key is getting to the root issue through high-tech biometrics and tackling situations through Fierce Conversations.

CHAPTER 6

TAKING ACTION THROUGH FIERCE CONVERSATIONS

What you're supposed to do when you don't like a thing is change it.

If you can't change it, change the way you think about it. Don't complain.

—Maya Angelou, *Wouldn't Take Nothing for My Journey Now*

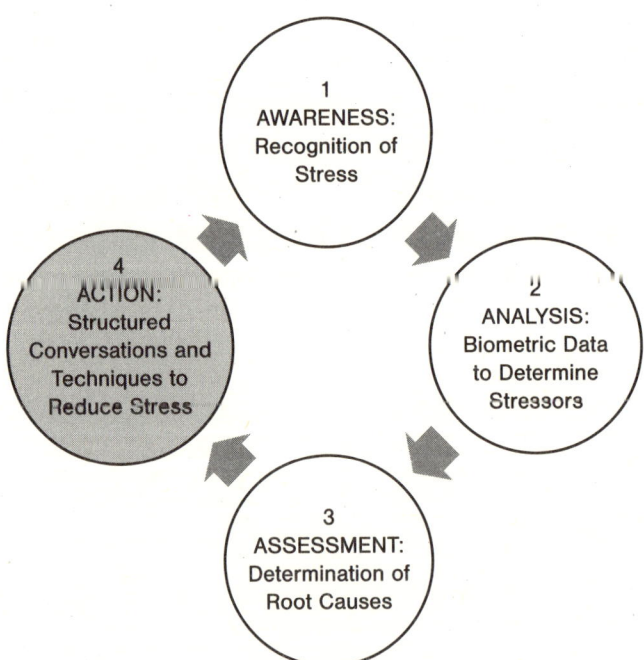

Figure 6.1. The Action Step

Y ou can take the power of Fierce Conversations and put it into action based on biometric intelligence. Fierce Conversations are essential to building individual and organizational resilience because they confront the sources of stress, defusing the communication snafus that are often responsible for problems in interactions. Each conversation confronts a source of stress, and with time and practice, you build Fierce Resilience.

THE ORIGIN OF FIERCE CONVERSATIONS

Susan Scott is my boss, mentor, and friend. In her spare time, she is also a best-selling author, speaker, and leadership-development expert known for her groundbreaking work in effective communication. Her career began in corporate training and consulting, where she gained extensive experience working with executives and leadership teams.

Her book *Fierce Conversations* became a pivotal work in communication and leadership. The book emphasizes the power of open, honest, and authentic conversations in fostering personal and professional growth and nurturing meaningful relationships. Susan wrote *Fierce Conversations* knowing that effective communication is the cornerstone of success in both professional and personal realms.

The book outlines practical strategies and principles to help readers navigate difficult conversations, confront challenging issues, and build stronger connections with others. She emphasizes the need to be fully present during conversations, listen deeply, and engage in courageous dialogue to uncover the truth and move toward positive outcomes. This idea changed the trajectory of both my personal and professional lives.

The book's inspiration came from her experiences and observations while working with various clients and leaders. She noticed that many individuals and organizations struggled with poor communication, which led to unresolved conflicts, inefficiency, and missed opportunities for growth. With a passion for helping people reach their potential, she wrote the book as a guide to empower individuals to transform their interactions, break down barriers, and foster authentic connections.

We need to be fully present during conversations, listen deeply, and engage in courageous dialogue to uncover the truth and move toward positive outcomes.

Throughout her career, Susan has continued to share her insights on effective communication and leadership through workshops, keynote speeches, and consulting services. Her work and our company have profoundly impacted countless individuals and organizations worldwide, helping them navigate challenging conversations and create a more transparent, accountable, and empowering culture.

For me, a Fierce Conversation is about stepping out from myself and engaging in authentic conversations. I know I'm having a Fierce Conversation when I speak with my true voice, addressing the heart of the matter, asking and listening genuinely, generating passion, enriching relationships, and experiencing personal growth by the end of the conversation.

Not easy, but immensely rewarding. Table 6.1 shares the seven principles of Fierce Conversations.

Table 6.1. The seven principles of Fierce Conversations

Principle	Description
1. **Master the courage to interrogate reality.**	To have Fierce Conversations, you must be willing to confront both your reality and that of others. They might not be the same. Once you have broadened your understanding of reality, then you're ready for truth-based conversation.
2. **Come out from behind yourself into the conversation and make it real.**	This requires shedding your defenses, setting aside your self-centered perceptions, withholding judgments, and ignoring distractions to be directly engaged with the other person and their reality.
3. **Be here, prepared to be nowhere else.**	Be fully present, giving your undivided and unfiltered attention to the person you are speaking with. When they realize they're truly being seen and heard, this fosters trust and creates a safe space for open dialogue.
4. **Tackle your toughest challenge today.**	A Fierce Conversation must address the most critical issues and challenges. No excuses. No procrastination. No kicking the can further down the road. Confront the most difficult topics first, clearing the way for real progress.
5. **Obey your instincts.**	Trust your instincts. Speak up when something feels off or when you sense there's an unspoken issue that needs immediate attention. Once you have mastered being present in the shared reality of that interaction, your instincts will tell you the truth.

continued

Table 6.1. Continued

Principle	Description
6. Take responsibility for your emotional wake.	Your words and actions impact others. You may be delivering solid advice, but it won't be received effectively if it's packaged in your hostility or judgment. Own what you leave behind when the conversation is over.
7. Let silence do the heavy lifting.	Silence is powerful in conversations. Allowing moments of silence gives space for reflection, deeper understanding, and processing of information. Resist the impulse to fill every pause in a conversation. Insight occurs in the space we leave between our words.

Source: Fierce Inc.

FIERCE CONVERSATION MODELS: A PRACTICAL AND GUIDED APPROACH

What drew me to Susan's work was how pragmatic and experiential it was. I read the theory and then practiced it. And I really did need to practice. I quickly understood that communication is a complex process that induces stress and anxiety in me, just like many individuals. Responsibilities such as giving or receiving feedback, confronting colleagues, expressing opinions, holding effective team meetings, and interacting with and influencing authority figures were challenging to navigate.

Using Susan's insights and Fierce Inc.'s own experience with thousands of people, we structured models to apply in various situations, guiding people to have meaningful and impactful dialogues, whether resolving conflicts, nurturing relationships, delegating effectively, or addressing difficult topics. You will see these models in action in part 2. They are the fourth component of the Fierce Resilience Cycle.

GOING AFTER CHALLENGING CONVERSATIONS

People tend to avoid conversations they think will be challenging, unaware that this avoidance leads to more stress and anxiety. Avoiding communication causes duplication of effort, mistakes, rework, and resentment and ultimately damages productivity, quality, and profitability. Fierce approaches teach how to courageously engage in those challenging conversations.

As I have discussed, *Fierce Conversations employs a systematic approach to reducing stress in the workplace by eliminating barriers to effective and authentic communication.* They help individuals build communication skills by providing a solid foundation of self-awareness and self-confidence. By breaking down effective communication into simple steps, these tools help guide people toward having meaningful and successful conversations throughout their careers and personal lives. When stress is addressed and resolved, productivity increases, and you build a fiercely resilient culture.

SEVEN CONVERSATIONS YOU NEED TO START HAVING TODAY

Sometimes you fail so slowly, you think you are doing fine. Your business may be failing one pointless conversation at a time. Do you struggle with missed sales targets? Are employees texting under the table during meetings? Do your high-level projects stall out?

The source of your problems is simpler than you think. It's conversation chaos. At your organization, it might go by another name: the echo chamber, business as usual, the same old story. The issue is communication that's unproductive, ineffective, and unfocused. Conversation chaos is more than frustrating. When your people don't know how to talk about what matters, it hurts your bottom line:

- You miss key insights because the whole team isn't participating.
- Toxic employees wreak havoc, and no one knows how to confront them.
- Leaders are overburdened and less effective because they don't delegate well.
- Discussions rehash the to-do list instead of diving into the heart of the matter.

There's more than one kind of conversation. In the twenty-plus years that we've been training people how to talk about what matters, we've pinpointed seven critical types of conversation. Each of these conversations, explained in table 6.2, is different and requires a unique approach to drive the most value.

THE POWER OF STORIES

You've probably noticed that I've used many stories in this book so far. I love a good story. Plus, I know that like a good conversation, a good story is a teaching moment. Research validates my thinking. Organizational psychologist Peg Neuhauser found that when a story is involved, learning is remembered more accurately and longer than just from facts and figures.[1] Research from psychologist Jerome Bruner suggests that facts are twenty-two times more likely to be remembered if they're part of a story.[2] Here are some stories to illustrate types of Fierce Conversations that represent the action component of the Fierce Resilience Cycle.

Table 6.2. Seven critical types of conversations

Conversation type	Description
1. Team	Helps teams make better and more inclusive decisions, shatters silos, increases collaboration, improves the ability to solve tough problems, and boosts buy-in across an organization.
2. Feedback	Transforms feedback sessions into candid, consistent, two-way conversations that spark lasting change.
3. Confrontation	Employs a straightforward conversation model that shifts attitudes, reduces tension, and enriches relationships by confronting unwanted tension and allowing people to come face-to-face with the truth.
4. Coaching	Uncovers solutions, prompts potent action, and unblocks professional paths.
5. Delegation	Clarifies roles, ends micromanagement, and puts people on a clear path of professional development.
6. Accountability	Moves teams from excuses to action by embracing responsibility, overcoming obstacles, and achieving everyday goals.
7. Negotiation	Enables people to foster the art of dealmaking and get to a solution that works for all by expanding thinking, examining competing perspectives, and embracing the opportunity hidden in every adversity.

Source: Fierce Inc.

Giving Feedback to a Stress-Inducing New Employee

A digital advertising agency needed help dealing with the assertive working style of a new team member, Henry, who talked and moved so fast that the team was getting stressed out. The situation showed hope for resolution once Elaine, a team member who was trained in the Fierce feedback framework, approached Henry after an especially tense meeting. He had no idea how the rest of the team felt and took the feedback to heart.

Timely feedback is essential to keeping resentment at bay and making calm, clearheaded conversations possible in the workplace. But many feedback discussions, no matter how well-intentioned, often start with judgments and accusations. It's no wonder that people try to avoid feedback or get defensive.

Rather than launch into criticism, a more effective way to begin these conversations is to provide a fact-based, objective example of what you observed, and then ask the other person to share their experience. This approach to communication is called *interrogating reality*, the idea that reality looks different to different people and that what we're perceiving isn't necessarily someone else's truth. This helps people recognize that their perspective is just that—their perspective, which is limited by many factors, including how much information they have. It encourages people to become curious about the views of others, a trait that doesn't come easily to most people, and to use that information to build a fuller picture of the situation.

Elaine provided examples of statements Henry had made during meetings without accusation or judgment and shared her thoughts and feelings in response to the statements. This enabled Henry to hear the feedback. And he expressed surprise and concern about the impact his actions were having—a more common reaction than our worst-case-scenario brains would have us think. In response, he explained the motivation for his intensity: Henry wanted the team to succeed. It also allowed him to reveal his stress and pressure and clear the air with everyone involved. This one conversation resolved the tension and strengthened the relationships among the entire team.

Helping a Stressed Dad

Alex, a busy dad with three children, found himself experiencing feelings of stress at work, even on days with no apparent issues or problems. He started receiving feedback and comments of concern about "not being fully present," "distant," and "disengaged, not focused." Using biometric intelligence, he gained valuable insights into his stress patterns and identified a significant source of stress: the morning routine of managing family obligations and getting the kids ready for school.

With the support of his coach, he recognized the importance of preparing the night before to ease the morning rush. Also, allocating an additional twenty minutes for the morning routine would allow for unexpected glitches in the process, reducing stress during this critical time. Moreover, Alex conversed with Lori, his significant other, to better balance expectations and shared responsibilities. This open dialogue, using the Feedback and Negotiation Models, enabled them to discuss specific tasks and balance household responsibilities more effectively.

As a result of these adjustments from self-awareness, Alex experienced an 18 percent increase in HRV, indicating reduced stress levels. People in his workplace also noticed a renewed energy, and he was back on track as a high performer. This newfound focus and self-awareness helped him tackle actual stress events throughout the day with a clearer and calmer mind. He would have more resilience going forward, built on biometric intelligence and targeted stress-management strategies.

Creating Psychological Safety in an Organization

A high-impact, knowledge-driven organization faced significant challenges as its knowledge workers were reluctant to speak up, leading to a lack of innovation and missed market opportunities. Through self-awareness exploration with Pulse and where stress was manifesting, leaders discovered the root cause of this issue: a clear lack of psychological safety within the organization. Employees feared repercussions and were apprehensive about expressing their thoughts and ideas. This created a general fear of failure, hindering collaboration and creativity.

To address this critical problem, they embarked on a focused cultural-change journey to create a safe and supportive environment for open communication using multiple conversational models. They provided coaching sessions that equipped individuals with the necessary tools and techniques to provide feedback in a secure, nonthreatening setting. They had open forum discussions that focused on empirical data from Pulse and insights from the cultural session. This not only helped get immediate buy-in instead of resistance, but these sessions also encouraged employees to express their thoughts, concerns, and ideas without fear of judgment or retribution.

During these coaching sessions, the organization identified a common thematic issue—the fear of losing their jobs and being perceived as inadequate in front of their peers and superiors. Armed with this knowledge, the organization consulted with its executive leadership to find comprehensive solutions to address these concerns effectively.

A boost in psychological safety can foster an environment of trust, empowerment, and engagement.

Within two weeks of implementing these changes, the organization observed a remarkable transformation in its workforce. The stress levels of employees significantly decreased, as evidenced by a 34 percent increase in HRV, indicating a reduction in stress levels. This boost in psychological safety fostered an environment of trust, empowerment, and engagement, resulting in improved collaboration, innovation, and a higher sense of purpose among employees. All of this added up to individual and organizational resilience that would help the organization move forward. This was now an embedded, accepted, and practiced part of its culture.

Resolving the Bleed-Over between Home Life and Work

Ella struggled to manage their stress effectively despite having attempted various traditional stress-management approaches, such as improving diet, sleep, meditation, and exercise. The root cause of the stress remained elusive until a detailed data analysis through Pulse revealed a significant bleed-over between their home life and work responsibilities.

Their data delineated between stress events in their home life and work life. Notably, stress levels were consistently higher during family-oriented events, such as date nights, caring for children, and family vacations. They initially believed that their home life was the primary source of stress, but through guided coaching sessions, Ella developed a deeper understanding of how the lines between home and work expectations had become blurred. Blame for stress is commonly misplaced and misunderstood.

The coaching process helped Ella gain self-awareness, leading to the realization that the stress experienced at home was impacting their performance and emotions throughout the day at work. The coach worked with them to establish clear boundaries between their professional and personal life, enabling them to maintain a healthy balance.

Through open and honest communication, they had delegation and feedback conversations with their boss and wife to create a better balance of expectations and shared responsibilities. By setting boundaries and clarity around availability and response times, they effectively reduced the stress bleed-over between home and work.

As a result, Ella reported an immediate 24 percent reduction in stress levels. This newfound self-awareness and proactive approach empowered them to navigate their professional and personal lives with a clearer sense of purpose and focus.

How Leadership Empowered a Participatory Culture

A company with a rich legacy of elevating lives through retirement, employee benefits, and life insurance solutions took on an ambitious project. Its goal was to not just talk the talk but truly walk the walk in promoting enhanced collaboration, inclusive communication, and integrating insights from every corner of the company. Here's the journey it embarked on:

- *Playing by the new rules*—It held engaging workshops where employees rolled up their sleeves and dove deep into the essence of the rules of engagement. The outcome was a workforce that felt connected, valued, and empowered to communicate effectively.
- *Running a manager bootcamp*—Every ship needs a skilled captain, right? The company believed in this and made sure its incoming leaders weren't just handed a rule book but were trained and equipped. New managers underwent a detailed onboarding process, ensuring they had the right tools and mindset to lead, mentor, and inspire their teams.

- *Broadening horizons*—Professional growth wasn't just about ticking off courses. The company looked at the bigger picture, emphasizing real-world applications, mentorship, and a culture of continuous learning.

Change isn't easy, especially when it's about altering deep-rooted behaviors. With its commitment and innovative approach, the company not only initiated change but made it a thriving part of the organizational culture. It showed that with the right tools and intent, conversations truly become a force for innovation and progress.

The most evident transformation was in the quality of conversations. Employees began speaking with courage and tact. The walls of hesitation crumbled, leading to richer dialogues and more innovative ideas. This wasn't about jargon but a shared understanding. Whether newbies or veterans were talking, there was a common thread of communication, ensuring everyone was on the same page.

One of the most heartening outcomes was the bridge between new employees and the old guard. The wealth of experience from long-term employees combined with fresh perspectives led to well-rounded decision-making. The way teams operated saw a positive shift, with more listening, understanding, and mutual support. Feedback became a two-way street, making it more holistic and constructive.

Rethinking Work-Task Preparation

Leticia, a senior manager at a global consultancy, was known for her high emotional intelligence and exceptional people-management skills. Despite this, she was experiencing persistent stress and anxiety, feeling that she had nothing new to learn.

Through thoroughly exploring Leticia's experiences and data analysis, Andrea, Leticia's coach, discovered common triggers that caused heightened stress levels during specific work tasks. Leticia coined this phenomenon as "lower in significance," where she noticed that particular tasks, although necessary, carried a disproportionate level of stress. She realized this kind of situation was a great candidate for the Delegation Model.

Another stressor for Leticia appeared in the data: she experienced spikes in anxiety and stress while preparing for high-stakes presentations. Surprisingly, during the presentations, she scored low on stress levels (one out of four), indicating a sense of thriving in those moments of performance. It was the prep time that was stressful.

Armed with these data-driven insights, Andrea helped Leticia develop deeper self-awareness and acknowledge that putting pressure on herself during preparation was a positive process that led to optimal results. With this newfound understanding, Leticia consciously decided to actively delegate tasks deemed as lower in significance, not only lightening her workload but also providing opportunities for her team members to grow and develop.

Furthermore, Leticia maintained a more composed mind during high-stakes presentations, resulting in lower physiological stress responses. As a result of these changes, her overall stress levels dropped by 15 percent. This case highlighted the transformative power of self-awareness and strategic delegation in managing stress and building resilience.

CREATE YOUR OWN STORY

Now that you have heard stories based on real examples, let's put you in the driver's seat with a self-reflection exercise in table 6.3 to help you identify your stress triggers and practice effective communication techniques to manage workplace stress.

Table 6.3. Fierce Conversations self-reflection

Steps	Explanation
1. Identify stress triggers.	Take time to reflect on recent situations that have caused stress at work. These triggers could be interactions with colleagues, feedback sessions, conflicts, or any other workplace situations that left you feeling stressed.
2. Analyze your reactions.	Consider how you reacted in the moment for each identified stress trigger. Did you become defensive, avoidant, or confrontational? Note your typical reactions.
3. Understand your emotional responses.	Dig deeper into your emotional responses during these stressful situations. Were you feeling anxious, angry, or overwhelmed? As you reflect back on them, are you conjuring a feeling? Understanding your emotions tied to these events will help you become more self-aware and prepared for future stressful encounters.
4. Identify communication challenges.	Identify any communication challenges you faced during these stressful situations. Did you struggle to express your thoughts clearly, listen actively, or assert your needs effectively?
5. Learn Fierce Conversation techniques.	Familiarize yourself with Fierce Conversation techniques in this book. These techniques focus on being honest, transparent, and authentic in communication.
6. Practice Fierce Conversations.	Choose one of the stressful situations you identified earlier and imagine having a Fierce Conversation. Prepare for and practice the conversation with a trusted colleague, friend, or coach.

continued

Table 6.3. Continued

Steps	Explanation
7. **Have a conversation.**	For example, to confront an issue, conduct a conversation aimed at • Clarifying the issue or concern • Identifying your emotions and those of the other person • Asking for the other person's perspective • Sharing your perspective with transparency • Finding common ground and potential solutions
8. **Get feedback.**	After role-playing the Fierce Conversation, seek feedback. Ask your partner to share their observations on your communication style, clarity, and effectiveness.
9. **Reflect on the experience.**	Reflect on the feedback you received. Consider what you did well and areas for improvement.

Source: Fierce Inc.

THE NEXT SECTION: CONVERSATION MODELS IN ACTION

The next part of this book focuses on situations in the workplace that specific conversation models can alleviate. This is the action component of the Fierce Resilience Cycle that you will see highlighted at the beginning of part 2.

The first three components of the Fierce Resilience Cycle (awareness, analysis, and assessment) do not lead to change without action. I will show you exactly how action applies to common situations that contribute to the stress that I have talked about so far. I have written this section so you see examples of what you can do and practice using the tools we have developed.

Just imagine if you could have structured conversations that would respond to issues like these:

- My employee is consistently showing up late and unprepared for meetings.
- My company tiptoes around problems instead of being transparent, open, and honest.
- Our feedback sounds more like criticism and tends to demotivate our teams.
- We don't feel safe confronting our managers when they are not living the organization's vision and values.
- I don't seem to be able to delegate. It backfired in the past, but I am completely swamped.
- I can't get out of my comfort zone, and it is hurting my career.
- My personal life is in shambles because of my work responsibilities.
- My team's productivity has plummeted.
- My organization doesn't understand or practice what inclusion means.

You can have these Fierce Conversations. It's time to walk the talk.

RESILIENCE REFRESHER

- Fierce Resilience is learned over time after repeated successful application of biometric data to stress management.
- The seven principles of *Fierce Conversations* are the vital fourth part of the Fierce Resilience Cycle action.
- Once stressful situations have been identified using biometric data, Fierce Conversation approaches are applied as stress busters and drive your desired results.
- Understanding the different conversation types helps you to determine how to have a structured conversation.

PART 2

PRACTICAL APPLICATIONS OF FIERCE RESILIENCE

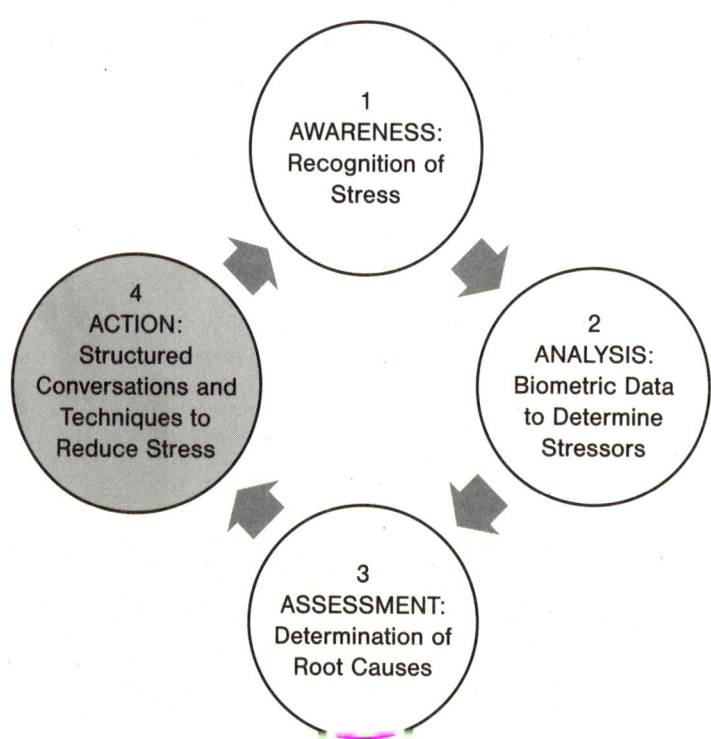

Figure II.1. The Action Step

CHAPTER 7

PUTTING FIERCE RESILIENCE INTO ACTION

I am lucky that whatever fear I have inside me, my desire to win is always stronger.

—SERENA WILLIAMS

The idea behind Fierce Resilience is that once you understand the root causes of stressors, with time and practice, you use Fierce Conversation models to improve your reaction, enrich your workplace, and prevent cumulative stress. You build resilience by facing challenges and learning from them. It's all about moving forward through action.

A Fierce Conversation is not just "Let's talk!" Practical conversation models need to be applied to workplace challenges. *These models map out the preparation and delivery of a constant flow of communication, which, over time, will build resilience by resolving stress and enriching relationships.*

In the following chapters, we'll look at the specifics of how to plan and hold these conversations, first with yourself and then with others in the workplace. I will be applying different conversation models to some of the top workplace challenges to demonstrate how they work:

- Giving and receiving feedback: Feedback Conversation Model
- Overcoming conflict: Confrontation Conversation Model
- Handling high-pressure conditions: Delegation Conversation Model
- Working outside your comfort zone: Accountability Conversation Model
- Maintaining work-life balance: Negotiation Conversation Model
- Responding to change: Team Conversation Model
- Building inclusion: Team Conversation Model
- Building culture: Values Conversation Model

DIGGING INTO A CHALLENGE

Before you start practicing with these models, let's get a feel for the structured approach you will be using throughout part 2. I'd like to take you through a universally applicable conversation tool that will help you discover the essential elements of a challenge, your personal role in it, and concrete plans for action.

This tool is called the Mineral Rights Exercise because you are mining for answers you need to own. This exercise is all about drilling down for the truth. This exercise includes the following seven steps:

1. Identify the issue.
2. Clarify the issue.
3. Determine its current impact.
4. Determine any future implications.
5. Examine your personal contributions to the issue.
6. Describe your ideal outcome.
7. Commit to action.

To illustrate what this might look like, let's take a look at an example challenge on building a new organizational culture devoted to Fierce Resilience. A conversation with yourself might play out like the one shown in table 7.1.

Table 7.1. An Example of a Mineral Rights Exercise

Steps	Example of a conversation with yourself
1. Identify the issue.	"My meetings are a disaster. No one will speak freely. Our decisions are creating subpar results."
2. Clarify the issue.	"We have weekly management meetings to discuss our current status and ongoing projects. Just top management comes, but I end up doing most of the talking. Everyone's on their phones or having side conversations. I want their input, but they seem to be afraid to jump into the discussion."
3. Determine its current impact.	"Since nobody else contributes ideas, I end up making decisions based on my own perspective. I feel like I have to do everything myself. And so far, that's not working; the most recent initiatives haven't met their goals, which is affecting the bottom line."
4. Determine any future implications.	"We're doomed. The profit arrow is pointing down and down. People are quitting in droves."
5. Examine your personal contributions to the issue.	"I'm definitely contributing to this problem. That's the hard part. I think I scare people when I get impatient and dominate the meetings. I did even fire one guy for speaking out aggressively against my plans. And I haven't gotten to know these people individually, so I don't know what their lives are like or how they see their future in the company. Yeah, I guess I have to take some blame for how the meetings go."

continued

Table 7.1. Continued

Steps	Example of a conversation with yourself
6. Describe your ideal outcome.	"I really would like to get their input. They have skills and perspectives that I don't have. I'd like them to feel like they can speak freely so we can work together on solutions. In fact, I'd like to make that kind of open communication a company habit. I know that we can do better on the bottom line if we can share ideas on how to do it."
7. Commit to action.	"I'm going to set a goal of sitting down with each of my people regularly and just letting them talk. Keep my mouth shut for a change. I want to get to know them and review the skills and ideas they bring to the table. And I need to structure our group meetings differently so each person has time to talk without fear of judgment. I'll run these meetings this way for three months, and then we'll check in to see if it's working. We can measure our success by increased meeting participation, employee retention, and effective project results."

Source: Fierce Inc.

As you see, the Mineral Rights Exercise is an inner conversation that I talked about in part 1 of the book. This honest discussion with yourself enables you to talk with others in the organization and understand what kind of conversational model works best. Mineral Rights is also used during coaching when you are exploring a challenge with other people. This helps you get to your root cause.

One last note before you dive deeper. If you are a leader in your organization, to have Fierce Resilience spread and gain the results you need for sustainable success, you need to lead by example.

That means taking action. Once your organization witnesses you actively practicing structured conversations, you will see profound change in the culture and in the lives of your employees. So keep a copy of this book on your desk. It will be worth it.

RESILIENCE REFRESHER

- Fierce Conversation models help you prepare and structure individual communications.
- The first conversation is with yourself.
- You lead by example.
- Transformation happens one conversation at a time.

CHAPTER 8

GIVING AND RECEIVING FEEDBACK
FEEDBACK CONVERSATION MODEL

I don't read reviews, but I do get feedback from my peers and people I know, like other actors and directors and producers.

—CHADWICK BOSEMAN

I love the following quote by Susan Scott about feedback: "Our careers, our companies, our personal relationships, and our very lives succeed or fail, gradually then suddenly—one conversation at a time."[1] Feedback is a conversation to help you and others stay awake during "gradually" so that we arrive at our desired "suddenly."

But what if those conversations don't happen?

If you've ever felt like you were working in a vacuum, navigating through a storm in the dark, you're not alone. The research is scary:

- 39 percent of employees report that they don't feel appreciated at work.
- Companies that implement regular employee feedback have 15 percent lower turnover rates.

- 43 percent of highly engaged employees receive feedback at least once a week—compared to only 18 percent of employees with low engagement.
- 65 percent of employees said they wanted more feedback, while 58 percent of managers think they give enough.
- 98 percent of employees will fail to be engaged when managers give little or no feedback.
- 69 percent of employees say they would work harder if they felt their efforts were being better recognized.
- 78 percent of employees said being recognized motivates them in their job.[2]

Viewing yourself objectively is extremely hard. You need feedback. Yet all of us avoid, deflect, and even fear the very conversations we need to progress toward our desired outcomes. And few leaders have ingrained frequent feedback into their communication practices with employees.

When you become resilient, you begin to reframe how you look at feedback to see without the blinders of fear. You see feedback as the fuel for that fierce bounce forward.

WHAT IS FIERCE FEEDBACK?

I like to define fierce feedback as a conversation in which you help yourself and others stay awake during "gradually" so you arrive at your desired "suddenly." Based on this definition, take a moment to think about these questions and how they relate to your organization:

- What price do you pay if you don't have a culture of feedback and feedback is not openly shared and received?

- What are the benefits of a feedback-rich culture where feedback is shared and received 365 days a year on your teams and with the people around you?

FEEDBACK CONVERSATION MODEL

The first transformational idea in Fierce Conversations is that your career and relationships succeed or fail, gradually then suddenly, one conversation at a time. You wake up at suddenly whether the occasion calls for celebration or bemoaning. But suddenlys don't happen every day. They're the big wins, the big fails.

The presence—or absence—of feedback contributes in a big way to your experience of suddenly. It's what happens—or doesn't happen—in the gradually that makes all the difference. If you have feedback waypoints along that gradual way, you're less likely to be surprised when you hit the suddenly of journey's end.

Your capacity to strengthen and enrich relationships and build performance is directly related to your ability to give, ask for, and receive feedback effectively, to help yourself and others stay awake during the "gradually."

UNDERSTANDING WAYPOINTS

The Feedback Conversation Model is based on the idea of waypoints. The term *waypoint* is commonly used to describe a physical point of reference in navigation, becoming far more widespread with the invention of handheld GPS, the maps on our phones, and that simulated voice you trust to guide you from place to place. Navigating careers, teams, and organizations is no different from navigating the road when you're driving: without markers along the way, you're destined to hear "Recalculating," "Make a U-turn," or "Return to the route." Feedback waypoints serve in the same way. They help you know where you are and where you are going. They help you get to your destination via the quickest and most effective route.

Fierce Resilience requires a continuous practice of learning from challenges and bouncing forward on the journey to your goals. You and your teammates are on that journey together. You're bound to lose your way sometimes, but that's part of what the team is there for: to pause you on your path with a wake-up call on your progress along the road.

Call that pause a waypoint, a check-in from your organizational GPS. You may need to recalculate, as GPS does when you take a wrong turn. Or that waypoint conversation may be a boost of encouragement, letting you know you're on the right track and suggesting further improvements by taking an alternate route to avoid the traffic ahead of you. Either way, feedback is a springboard for your bounce forward.

Feedback is essential to achieve success in both personal and professional life. *The presence or absence of feedback affects our ability to adapt to changes.* Feedback is a conversation that acts as a guiding force on our journey toward our goals. Like navigational waypoints, feedback waypoints help us identify our current location and the direction we need to head toward.

If you think of your destination as a desired suddenly or a particular goal or outcome you want to reach, think of waypoints as the conversations that had the input, candor, wisdom, and encouragement of others along the way.

COMPONENTS OF THE FEEDBACK CONVERSATION MODEL

The Feedback Conversation Model has three main components, as seen in table 8.1.

Table 8.1. The Feedback Conversation Model components

Component	Description
Experience	Lay out the when, where, and what of the behavior you have observed. What was *your* experience? Be specific. Describe a specific when, where, and what. Use concrete examples. Eradicate vague references, loaded words, and assumptions.
Explore	Invite the other person's perspective. Get curious about when, where, and what. Ask, "What's true for *you*? What was *your* experience? How do *you* see this? Can you tell me what was going on? I'm curious if . you see what I see."
Explain	Why is this conversation or this feedback essential? Why does it matter? What are the results if this behavior continues? What is the impact if nothing changes? Think of the impacts for them, you, the team, and the organization.

Source: Fierce Inc.

When using the Feedback Model, doing some preparation can be helpful. Look in the mirror and start with yourself. Check your context for giving feedback. Ask yourself the following questions:

- What is my true intention with giving feedback? Do I want to improve performance, to work better together, or to be right?
- Am I making assumptions about the person and their abilities, decisions, and behaviors? Interrogate your reality. Are those assumptions based on fact, hearsay, or prejudice?

- Have I laid out my expectations for this person in clear and direct terms?
- Have I set realistic goals with this person?

CASE STUDY: WDS PROMOTES FEEDBACK IN ITS COMPANY

The top brass at Washington Dental Service (WDS), a large dental practice, were on the hunt to craft an environment that was more transparent, open, and honest. Like in many places, real talk was hard to come by. People were often tiptoeing around issues instead of diving in with genuine heart and guts. Larry Marino, a training guru at WDS, summed it up: "Imagine only talking about problems during performance reviews. That's what was happening. No daily check-ins, no building trust. It was like saving all the drama for season finales."

WDS is the top provider of dental benefits in Washington, ensuring sparkling smiles for over half a century. But it wanted leaders who not only led but also inspired others to step up. It aimed for a culture where employees felt empowered, owning up to their roles and responsibilities. The big question was how to bring about this change without messing with the customer experience.

Fierce teamed up with WDS to use the Feedback Conversation Model. After all training was done, Jim Dwyer, the big boss at WDS, noticed people were happier. He shared, "The vibes are better. There's more confidence in feedback sessions and challenging chats."

Marino echoed this sentiment: "Instead of holding out for review time, people are chatting, clarifying, and coaching every day. The result? Everyone feels seen and heard."

ASKING FOR FEEDBACK

When and where should you ask for feedback? You don't want to catch your counterpart off guard or distracted. Plan for a time and place that you think you can have their full attention. Before your meeting, ask yourself these questions based on the Feedback Conversation Model:

- *Experience*—What is one of your desired goals or objectives?
- *Explore*—From whom do you need feedback along the way? Why that person?
- *Explain*—What results are you currently getting, and where can you improve?

Write out your responses in two to three sentences. Here are some examples:

- *Experience*—"When I lead a meeting, my goal is to have a robust, transparent conversation with everyone so that we understand and respect one another's perspectives."
- *Explore*—"I would appreciate hearing from you about ways in which I could have improved the experience and outcomes of the meeting."
- *Explain*—"I ask because it's easy for me to assume the meeting is going well, but there is always room for improvement."

RECEIVING FEEDBACK

I have found that receiving feedback is often more difficult than giving it. It requires an open mind and, most importantly, the ability to listen. Again, take a structured approach to receiving feedback. This is where having inner conversations with yourself is valuable.

- *Experience*—Look for the what, when, and where.
  - Listen carefully to what's being said and how.
  - Say, "Thank you."
  - Decide what you can learn from the feedback.
- *Explore*—Get curious.
  - First, be curious and genuinely open to learning.
  - Ask for clarification and specific examples. Ask when and where you have been observed doing that behavior. For how long has it been going on? What is the impact of that behavior on them, the team, and the organization?
- *Explain*—Clarify why it matters.
  - Take responsibility for the impact, and present your thoughts.
  - Reiterate gratitude for the feedback, and share why it is important to you.
  - Articulate your future focus.

GIVING PRAISE

Positive feedback is important for growth. That means you need to know how to give and receive praise. Follow the same structure from the Feedback Conversation Model:

- *Experience*—Look for the where, when, and what.
  - When and where did you observe the behavior?
  - Give specifics and details.
  - Saying "Good job" is not enough.
- *Explore*—Get curious.
  - Ask questions that help you incorporate the feedback.
  - Have you received feedback like this before?
  - Where does this land for you in your map of where you are and where you're going?

- *Explain*—Clarify why it matters.
  - Articulate why they deserve to hear this feedback.
  - Tell how it impacts you and others in the best of ways.

CASE STUDY: **EMILY'S STORY**

Emily, an account executive at a prestigious advertising agency, was known for her dedication and creativity. However, she tended to take criticism to heart, often feeling discouraged by the slightest feedback.

One day, Emily received an email from her account director, Ben, requesting her presence in his corner office. She had butterflies in her stomach as she walked down the corridor to his office, speculating what might be the reason for the sudden meeting. When she entered, Ben gestured for her to take a seat. "Emily, I wanted to talk to you about your recent project, the Sunrise Café campaign. Overall, it was excellent work, very creative and well-executed."

Emily's heart soared with relief, thinking that maybe she had done everything perfectly this time. She smiled and nodded, waiting for more praise. Ben continued, "I have to say, I'm impressed with your work. Keep it up." That was it: no specific feedback or suggestions for improvement, just a brief acknowledgment of her work. Emily left the meeting feeling somewhat confused. She had expected feedback, something to help her grow and improve, but it seemed like everything was fine.

Over the next few weeks, Emily continued to work on various projects, including the Sunrise Café campaign. She felt complacent, thinking her work was already perfect since her boss hadn't pointed out any areas for improvement. When the client saw the proposed campaign, they expressed serious concerns about the color palette and messaging. Emily was taken aback. She thought her creative team had nailed it. She had heard no criticism or suggestions for improvement from her boss, so the client's disappointment was a total surprise.

The lack of feedback had left Emily unaware of potential improvements she could have made. Ben and the organization's management had not realized that they were responsible for designing the company's communication culture. Without a feedback culture, Emily's project, once promising, became a missed opportunity for Emily and the agency. Emily's stress rose as she struggled to grow and adapt to changing industry trends. The company was delivering subpar work to its clients and began to see a steep decline in profitability.

The shift to a feedback culture had to happen. Ben hit a painful suddenly when he learned of the agency's failure with the Sunrise Café client. He had failed to provide Emily with the feedback that would have redirected her toward a more client-focused campaign.

As a leader, he had an accountability conversation with himself, realizing that he had an opportunity to lead the agency in a transformation into a feedback culture. Ben opened the next meeting by holding himself accountable for not providing Emily with the needed feedback on Sunrise Café. "I recognize that I did not give you the feedback you needed to adjust and conclude the campaign successfully. The agency is a fast-paced environment, and feedback is essential. When it is vague or missing altogether, we can find ourselves confused and stressed. I want to correct this moving forward. I would like to give you some feedback on Hipster Boutique."

Emily nodded but already felt her heart beating faster. She wondered how this would go. Ben began by sharing his experience: "Yesterday, during our meeting for the Hipster Boutique campaign, I was impressed with the progress to date; your color palette is spot on. There are a few areas that could be even better."

Emily nodded, palms sweating as she braced herself for criticism. Ben continued, "Can you explain the font choice?"

"I have yet to land on a font style; I was waiting to ask for your feedback. Do you have any suggestions?" Emily asked.

"Yes, thank you for asking. Exploring a more modern font will better align with the boutique's image. Also, while the copywriting was engaging, we could refine the messaging to better connect with their target audience."

As he continued with his feedback, Emily listened carefully, jotting notes as always. To her surprise, he wasn't tearing the work apart but was providing constructive suggestions to enhance it. They had an open and honest discussion about improvements, rather than negative critiques.

Once the meeting concluded, Emily thanked Ben for his feedback and left his office feeling relief and gratitude. She realized this was a thoughtful discussion aimed at helping her grow as a professional. Over the next few weeks, Emily implemented the changes with her team, choosing a more contemporary font that perfectly complemented the campaign and reworking the copy to make it more relatable to the target audience.

Emily presented the campaign to the client; they were thrilled with the improvements and signed off on it without any reservations. The Hipster Boutique campaign became a major success, garnering attention from the industry and the public.

Emily's newfound confidence in receiving feedback had a profound impact on her work and career. She began seeking out feedback from colleagues and actively seeking growth opportunities. The feedback sessions transformed Emily into a more resilient and growth-oriented professional. She learned that constructive feedback was not a judgment of her abilities but a waypoint to improvement and success.

Ben continued his journey toward infusing the agency's culture with a 365-day feedback practice. He scheduled face-to-face check-in meetings with his employees on a regular basis and set that precedent for all other company leaders. No feedback opportunity was left behind.

RESILIENCE REFRESHER

- Feedback is a conversation in which you help yourself and others stay awake during gradually so that you arrive at your desired suddenly.
- Waypoints are the conversations you need along the way to navigate successfully toward your desired suddenlys.
- Every aspect of feedback—giving, asking, and receiving—has three components: experience (the when, where, and what), explore (being curious, interrogating reality, and provoking learning), and explain (the why and what next).
- It takes courage to give feedback. Saying "thank you" ensures the feedback continues.

CHAPTER 9

OVERCOMING CONFLICT
CONFRONTATION CONVERSATION MODEL

In case of dissension, never dare to judge till you've heard the other side.

—Euripides

Most of us naturally shy away from conflict. It's stressful and threatening. You feel your blood pressure spiking just anticipating those verbal fisticuffs and flying emotional sparks. Your fight-or-flight reflexes say, "Duck! Dodge! Disengage! Run for cover!" Conflict is stressful. We've covered the costs of stress in part 1, and of course nobody wants to feel stressed. But we've also talked a lot about how to build Fierce Resilience. Remember the fourth principle of Fierce Conversations—tackle your toughest challenge today—from chapter 6? That's what I'm talking about here. Facing conflict. Growing resilience.

YOU ARE NOT ALONE

If you experience conflict at work—occasionally, weekly, or even daily—research shows that you are not alone:

- 80 percent of people say managing difficult relationships is the reason for quitting. To put that in perspective, $600 billion a year is lost in employee turnover.
- 42 percent of people reported that yelling and other verbal abuse was common in their work environment.
- *In a survey of five thousand full-time employees in nine different countries, 85 percent of employees dealt with conflict at work to some degree, and 29 percent dealt with conflict frequently or always.*[1]

THE CONFRONTATION MODEL

Let's look at the Confrontation Conversation Model and the thinking behind it. First, all confrontation is the search for the truth. We each have a different perspective of what's going on, and we both want to know what the reality is. After all, we're on the same team, and we've both committed to the company's goals. If we arrive at a shared perception, we can go forward toward those goals together. Furthermore, confronting behavior or issues with the other person is more helpful than going into the conversation with a plan to confront the person. This perspective helps open up a higher likelihood of successful outcomes.

CASE STUDY: FROM CONFLICT TO CONVERGENCE

Placido was a data analyst in a large tech company with an intense work environment. Placido's manager, Ed, was a demanding and critical boss known for his lack of empathy and approachability.

"We're all scared of this guy," said Placido. "When he pushes ideas that we don't think are in line with our company goals, and that's pretty often, we just hide behind our computer monitors. We'd like to confront him, but none of us feel safe."

In the context of this stressful workplace, Placido discovered a potential data breach that could have severe consequences if not addressed promptly. Placido mustered the courage to raise the issue during a team meeting, hoping to initiate a solution-focused discussion. Ed reacted with hostility, dismissing Placido's concerns and belittling him in front of the team, eroding his self-esteem and further discouraging others from speaking up.

Placido felt disheartened by Ed's response, questioning his own abilities and regretting bringing up the issue. He reached out to his coach, Alexa, for guidance.

The Preparation

Alexa reminded Placido of their in-house training in Fierce Conversations. She highlighted the importance of tackling the tough challenges and encouraged Placido to confront the issue; however, she told him, "This is not a conversation you want to wing. Take some time to prepare an opening statement, the first sixty seconds of the conversation." This would allow Placido to articulate his perspective clearly and succinctly.

Alexa recommended that Placido use the Confrontation Model to prepare for his meeting with Ed. She told him that the opening statement would probably be about the first sixty seconds of the conversation. First, he needed to walk himself through an analysis of the problem and plan his opening statement as outlined in table 9.1.

As expected, Ed at first reacted defensively, not unlike how many of us would when facing confrontation. This reaction can come in one of several ways:

Deny: "It wasn't me!" or "It never happened!"
Defend: "It wasn't my fault, it was because of . . ."
Deflect: "It's not about this, it's about . . ."

Table 9.1. How to develop an opening statement

Step	Prompt	Placido's example
1. Name the issue.	"I want to talk with you about the effect [the issue] is having on [what/whom]."	"I want to talk with you about the effect your leadership style is having on the team."
2. Select a specific example that illustrates the behavior or situation that you want to change.	"For example, . . ."	"For example, when I brought up the potential data breach, you dismissed my concerns with what appeared to be a condescending tone in front of the team."
3. Describe your emotions around the issue.	"I feel . . ."	"I feel embarrassed, discouraged, and highly concerned."
4. Clarify why it's important, what is at stake to gain or lose for you, for others, for the team, for the organization.	"From my perspective, the stakes are high. X is at stake, and most importantly, Y is at stake."	"For me, this team, and this company, a great deal is at stake. I'm unsure I want to continue with a company where people are afraid to speak up, or if they do, they experience major repercussions. The morale of the team is at stake, and just as important, the company could lose client confidence and revenue if this potential breach is not addressed."

continued

Table 9.1. Continued

Step	Prompt	Placido's example
5. Identify your contribution to the problem.	"I realize my fingerprints are on this. I have [action or inaction]. And I want to apologize."	"I recognize that I didn't bring my concerns to you earlier, and for this, I apologize."
6. Indicate your wish to resolve this issue.	"I want to resolve with you [restate the issue]."	"I want to resolve this with you—the effect your leadership style is having on the team."
7. Invite your partner to respond.	"I sincerely want to hear your perspective. Please talk with me."	"Can we talk candidly together about this? I want to hear your perspective."

Source: Fierce Inc.

But Placido held his ground and maintained his composure, remaining professional yet sharing his personal perspective, reaffirming their mutual commitment to the company's goals and emphasizing the need for a healthy, psychologically safe work environment. Ed's attitude softened, and he showed willingness to engage in authentic conversation.

The Interaction

The next phase of the Confrontation Conversation Model takes the most time. In this example, invited to express his perspective, Ed gets a chance to reflect on his behavior. Placido had offered specific examples of incidents that Ed himself had witnessed and participated in, so their discussion was based on that shared reality. Ed reflected on his behavior and acknowledged the validity of

Placido's concerns, revealing some personal stressors that contributed to his reaction.

The two engaged in an open conversation and together built a resolution to improve communication and psychological safety within the team. Placido modeled the listening techniques of paraphrasing and checking in with the other person's perception. They both then dug for a full understanding of the other's perception and interests. Most importantly, they reaffirmed their mutual commitment to the company's goals and to growing an open, healthy communication practice in the work environment.

The Resolution

Before ending the meeting, the two clarified what they had learned and where they stood after this conversation. Was anything left unsaid that still needs saying? They set down their new understanding. They made concrete plans for how to move forward, given this new understanding. And they made a clear agreement on a method to hold one another accountable to achieve it.

Placido's courage to confront the issue inspired other team members to start speaking up, gradually shifting the workplace culture. Ed's newfound openness modeled a new communication culture for the organization, one where constructive, all-around feedback was a daily practice, and all members touched base often to reaffirm their common goals and elucidate their diverse perspectives.

PRACTICE THE CONFRONTATION CONVERSATION MODEL

Now it's your turn to practice the Confrontation Model using the following five steps:

1. *What do you need to confront?* Confirm that this confrontation is necessary. If this problem has occurred only once so far, it might call for a Feedback Conversation instead. In that case, go back to the Feedback Conversation in chapter 8.

2. *What do you feel?* Your emotions are important here because most decisions are based on emotions and then rationalized later. And if this situation does call for a confrontation, you may be headed for decisions that affect your career and your company.

3. *Plan your opening statement.* Avoid these common confrontation opening errors:

   - Don't start with "How's it going?" Be real. You're not here to shoot the breeze. And you know how it's going; that's why you're having this conversation.

   - Don't sugarcoat it. Many of us have been taught to start with something positive, but don't. That's a separate conversation. Do one conversation at a time.

   - Don't cushion your real point with vague statements. Get right to your plan.

   - Don't write the script of the interaction. You might expect a certain response, probably negative, but you don't know how this will go. Let the conversation become what it becomes.

   - Don't come on like a wrecking ball. Aggressive presentation invites retreat or fighting. Just state your case calmly and clearly. Get right to the point in neutral language. Focus on enriching the relationship. You should go into this conversation with the expectation that real change can occur as a result.

4. During the interaction phase, apply the seven principles of Fierce Conversations.

5. Make the resolution phase a clear, specific road forward:
    *   Reaffirm what's agreed upon and where you agree to disagree.
    *   Clearly define the actions you both plan to take to implement the agreement.
    *   Decide on a method to check in on your progress going forward.

WHEN TO USE THE FEEDBACK MODEL VERSUS THE CONFRONTATION MODEL

You will need to know when to use the Confrontation Model versus the Feedback Model from the previous chapter. The Confrontation Model is used only after the Feedback Model is used but does not work.

Let's compare the two to get a better understanding of when they should be used, as seen in table 9.2.

FEEDBACK OR CONFRONTATION MODEL: YOU DECIDE

Read through the following story and determine if you should use the Feedback Model or Confrontation Model. Your decision should be based on table 9.2.

Heather had a mentee, Lisa, whose negative attitude and behavior created an unpleasant work environment for colleagues and administrative staff. Heather described her as complaining about everything. As a more seasoned teacher, you want to help with advice, so we did repeatedly." Initially, colleagues provided feedback to help the Lisa deal with the issues she complained about. She made no attempts at change, so the advice was being ignored.

Table 9.2. When to use the Feedback Model versus the Confrontation Model

When to use the Feedback Model	When to use the Confrontation Model
• The problem has never happened before, and you don't think the other person was aware they did it. • They did a great thing, and you want to make sure they know how much it means to you, the team, and the company. • You see a pattern that could become a problem for this person later on, and you want them to have a chance to see it when they have time to course-correct. • This problem has just happened once, and there's no need to change now, but you do want them to see it from your different perspective. • A mistake was made, and sharing perspectives on how it could have been done better is important.	• A pattern of similar behavior has been established and addressed before, but nothing has changed or is not changing quickly enough. • They did something that is troublesome to you, the team, or the organization, and it shouldn't happen again. • The individual has done something, and once is too much. • It keeps happening, and now it affects your relationship, your ability to work effectively together, or the overall results. • Mistakes keep being made, and an underlying issue needs to be corrected to prevent further unanticipated mistakes.

Source: Fierce Inc.

Heather was aware of the situation, and for the sake of her coworkers and mentee, she decided to structure the critical but challenging conversation about Lisa's attitude and behavior at work. "I explained the impact of her behavior, and let her know what I felt about the situation. I then shared the behavioral expectations for continued employment. The behavior needed to stop."

Heather was willing and able to have this meaningful conversation with Lisa, who was receptive to the input. "She was thanking me at the end of the conversation. She said, 'That was exactly what I needed to hear, and thank you.'" The conversation also helped to strengthen their relationship. Heather reports, "I gained even more of her trust because something deep inside people really responds to being leveled with."

If you determined this was a case for using the Confrontation Model, you are correct.

Confrontation is about as stressful as it gets, even if it's done over a conference table with coffee and cookies. Done fiercely, though, confrontation is grounds for growth and enriched relationships. No more hiding behind your computer monitor.

RESILIENCE REFRESHER

- Confrontation is for urgent matters.
- Confrontation is an opportunity for clarification and realignment of goals.
- A fierce confrontation opening statement is carefully planned.
- Confrontation is all about taking action.

CHAPTER 10

HANDLING HIGH-PRESSURE CONDITIONS

DELEGATION CONVERSATION MODEL

It's not about how hard you hit. It's about how hard you can get hit and keep moving forward.

—ROCKY BALBOA

Indra Nooyi was the CEO of PepsiCo from 2006 to 2018. She faced numerous challenges in leading one of the world's largest food and beverage companies.[1] Recognizing that the demands of the role were immense and to sustain the company's growth and navigate a rapidly changing industry, she needed to manage her time and energy more efficiently. Delegation became a key strategy for her stress relief and enhanced productivity.

In interviews and speeches, Nooyi often shared her approach to delegation and how it contributed to her ability to manage stress. One notable example is how she empowered her leadership team to take charge of specific aspects of the business. She believed in hiring strong individuals and giving them the autonomy to make decisions within their areas of expertise.

Nooyi entrusted her team with responsibilities ranging from product innovation and marketing to supply-chain management and international operations. By doing so, she not only distributed the workload but also fostered a culture of accountability and collaboration within the company.

This approach allowed Nooyi to focus on the most critical strategic aspects of leading PepsiCo, such as navigating global market trends, establishing sustainability initiatives, and driving long-term growth. By delegating operational and day-to-day tasks, she dedicated more time to shaping the company's future and maintaining a healthy work-life balance.

The result was not only a successful period for PepsiCo but also a less stressed and more fulfilled CEO. Indra Nooyi's story highlights the importance of effective delegation in corporate leadership, demonstrating that trusting and empowering a capable team leads to better stress management and overall success for both the leader and the organization.

LEADERS NEED TO DELEGATE

How many times have you heard a boss complain, "Why do I *always* have to do everything *myself*?" For me, this statement would most often come from a person who didn't know or trust their team. Sometimes, that lack of trust was well-founded, but usually, it wasn't. Those bosses were feeling pressure that they had created for themselves by not communicating with their people.

One common scenario revolves around delegation. Often, employees assume that managers have a clear understanding of the work they've delegated. However, managers are also busy and may not have a complete view. *The Delegation Conversation Model teaches employees to proactively engage in discussions with their managers about workload and priorities.* This helps avoid overwhelming feelings and promotes better communication, greatly reducing stress and misunderstandings in the workplace.

Learning how to delegate requires knowing the skills required by each item on your to-do list, learning the skills of your workforce, finding the courage to give up the reins, and planning for follow-ups. A leader's effective delegation is a keystone of Fierce Resilience: it's built on honest communication, commitment to shared goals, clear and consistent feedback, and clearly allocated accountability. The goal of delegation is to develop individuals. It involves assigning levels of responsibility and reporting, not just tasks, and is determined per individual person, not per job title.

Handling high-pressure situations and delegation are the twin pillars on which effective leadership is forged. In times of great pressure, true leaders rise to the occasion, displaying unwavering composure and clarity of purpose. They understand that the art of delegation becomes their most potent weapon amid chaos.

Delegation is not relinquishing control but rather a strategic distribution of responsibility, enabling a team to function as a cohesive force. This act is the hallmark of a leader's trust in their team's abilities and an affirmation of collective strength. The ability to manage high-pressure situations while skillfully delegating tasks is a testament to a leader's resilience and strategic acumen, ensuring survival and triumph in the face of adversity.

Ask yourself, Why don't I delegate? List your reasons, and then determine your number one internal obstacle to delegation.

CASE STUDY: LET GO TO HOLD ON

John is the CEO of a growing security company. As part of the intelligence community, he is no stranger to high-pressure conditions. He had climbed the corporate ladder, driven by a relentless work ethic and an intense determination to succeed. The company has seen unprecedented growth over the past three years thanks to his visionary leadership and a remarkable team.

However, John had a secret struggle that gnawed at him—a reluctance to delegate. In the past, the wrong delegation decisions had cost him.

His fear was not that the board would criticize him; he would weather that storm with his experience. Instead, the prospect of his juniors facing the brunt of the consequences haunted him. He didn't want to carry the weight of their mistakes negatively impacting their careers.

John's internal conflict had reached a boiling point, manifesting as a panic attack. It was a wake-up call for John. He realized he needed to change his approach to pressure, recalibrate his mindset, and reset his relationship with his team. The high-pressure conditions weren't going away, and he understood that his team's collective potential was the key to enduring success.

John thought about what was preventing him from being a more effective delegator. He recognized that his hesitation stemmed from a lack of trust and a misguided sense of responsibility. He needed to redefine his role and the roles of his team members. It was time to establish clear boundaries and responsibilities.

John learned a new approach to making delegation decisions using the Delegation Conversation Model. One of its key components is called the *fierce decision tree*. This tool is not the yes/no decision flowchart that you might be familiar with; rather, it uses the parts of a tree to simply indicate where individuals have decision-making rights to take action with each of their responsibilities. Effectively using a decision tree leads to direct outcomes: an individual's development path becomes clear, their progress is acknowledged, and leaders are free to lead instead of micromanage. The decision tree is a tool for delegation that lays out four different levels of delegation: leaf, branch, trunk, and root.

- *Leaf*—At this highest level, individuals are empowered to make decisions independently without needing to report back to John. They own these responsibilities completely.
- *Branch*—Decisions at this level require the individual to make the call and report to John regularly. This allows him to stay informed.
- *Trunk*—Here, decisions need to be made by the individual, but they have to report back to John before acting. This gives him the chance to provide input.
- *Root*—These decisions can't be delegated or should be made collaboratively with input from many people. The ultimate decision rests with John.

With this framework fully ingrained, John embarked on a journey of effective delegation. He invited Jan, a trusted team member, to an upcoming strategy-planning session. They needed to make a critical decision during the session, one for which John knew he couldn't be present for all the details. "I'm going to give you this responsibility at the trunk level," John said to Jan. "Make the decision, but before you act, let me know what you've decided and how you arrived at that decision. I may have some changes, but I want a decision, not a suggestion." The strategy-planning session went smoothly, and Jan successfully implemented the decision, reporting back to John as instructed.

Later that week, John met with Jan to discuss an onboarding client whose needs had many moving parts. Jan thought her role would be like every other time: John would require sign-off on her decisions. But, to her surprise, he said, "You've shown me that you make great decisions in this area, so I would like you to take the responsibility on this one at the branch level. Make the decision, take action, and we can discuss it at our regularly scheduled check-in."

John was satisfied with his own success at delegation. Jan felt pride as she accepted this new level of responsibility and saw her own upward progression. "Thank you, John. I'll update you on our progress and make decisions aligning with our vision."

Over time, Jan learned to manage high-pressure conditions and flourish in her role. John became even more confident in delegating responsibilities to her, and their working relationship became more efficient. To his surprise, John found he had more time to focus on strategic matters requiring his attention.

One day, as John reviewed the company's operations, he came across a project he had previously managed personally. He realized that Jan could now take complete ownership of it. When he met with her, John said, "I will give you this responsibility at the leaf level. You've proven that you make well-thought-out, strategic decisions. It's all yours!"

Thanks to that essential wake-up call, John learned the benefits of delegation. His stress levels decreased, he discovered how capable Jan was, and together, they managed the high-pressure conditions successfully.

PRACTICE USING THE DECISION TREE

First, let's look at the following profile about Kyle, then practice using the decision tree on his situation:

- Kyle is a great employee. They have been on your team for eighteen months and have shown a lot of initiative. They're highly motivated and respected by their peers.
- Your concern about Kyle is that they are becoming too comfortable where they are. You are worried you could lose Kyle unless you find ways to challenge them.

- Currently, Kyle does a great job running their weekly meetings. They've been doing it for a while, they follow through consistently, and no issues have arisen from their weekly team meetings. They've been inviting you to the meetings and copying you on meeting action items. You have complete confidence in Kyle and don't feel you need to be involved.
- You expect Kyle to continue to update the stakeholders, but you want to be aware of all communication with them so you're not blindsided by anything.
- Kyle has been maintaining the budget for over six months. You need them to make recommendations as to how the department can save 5 percent across the board due to a mandatory 5 percent overall reduction in budget. You're interested in their suggestions but would like to talk it over with them before you implement anything.
- Strategic planning is coming up. You'd love to have Kyle's input at that meeting. They're innovative, so you'll invite them to attend.

For the following indicated job responsibilities, assign each to Kyle at root, trunk, branch, or leaf level according to how you plan to delegate:

Update stakeholders: _____ level
Conduct weekly meetings: _____ level
Annual strategic planning: _____ level
Make budget recommendations: _____ level

As you elevate Kyle's decision-making responsibility, how much of your pressure have you relieved? How do you think your delegation decisions will affect Kyle's engagement and career path?

DELEGATING YOURSELF

It would be great to do the following exercise with a partner. Make it a Fierce Conversation, taking turns in roles of listener or interviewer and leader or delegator. Think about a responsibility on your plate that you would like to delegate. Determine at what decision tree level you are going to delegate this responsibility.

Ask your partner the following questions in the order given. As always, probe to dig deeper. If you're answering the questions, get creative. Switch roles to give your partner a chance to practice delegating.

1. What would be the best use of your time for this current or new responsibility?
2. What activity or responsibility is no longer the best use of you? Of course it's important to the organization, and you're good at it, but do you need to still do it yourself?
3. To whom would you like to give this responsibility?
4. At what level, leaf, branch, or trunk?
5. By when?
6. How much of your time will this free up?

RESILIENCE REFRESHER

- Clearly identify which categories various decisions and actions fall into so that an individual knows exactly where they have the authority to make decisions and act.
- Provide employees with a clear and upward path of professional development. Progress is made when decisions and actions are moved from root to trunk to branch to leaf categories.
- Create a culture where everyone in the organization takes full responsibility for their actions.

CHAPTER 11

WORKING OUTSIDE YOUR COMFORT ZONE

ACCOUNTABILITY CONVERSATION MODEL

You must do the thing you think you cannot do.

—ELEANOR ROOSEVELT

In our work worlds, there are times when we need to take on new responsibilities and times when we need to assign those responsibilities to someone who doesn't feel ready to take them on. This boils down to accountability—to interrogating reality, clarifying goals, listening, and acting. We need to have honest conversations with ourselves and others. We need courage.

Comfort zones, those reassuring psychological constructs that wrap us in familiarity and security, represent the essence of feeling safe, unchallenged, and in control. Yet in this cozy realm, personal growth and self-discovery remain elusive. The formidable act of breaking free from our own comfort zones sparks profound psychological transformation.

Confronting fear, uncertainty, and the inevitable discomfort often elicits anxiety and resistance. Paradoxically, the seeds of genuine growth and self-improvement germinate within this discomfort. Growth requires taking account of our current situation, revisiting our goals, and assessing our waypoints on our own journeys.

This potent journey evokes a fundamental psychological principle, the Yerkes-Dodson law, which identifies a zone of optimal arousal and stress for peak performance.[1] While comfort zones offer low-stress levels, only by venturing into the *optimal anxiety zone*, where moderate stress resides, can individuals and organizations unlock the potential for performance and personal growth.

JO'S STORY: FROM COMFORT ZONE TO GROWTH ZONE

Jo had spent her entire life within her comfort zone, adhering to a familiar routine. She had pursued education, married, and raised children, all in the same town where she had grown up. She had built a stable life, but its trajectory was flat. Jo had plodded along, reassuring herself that this predictability was comforting.

In her late forties, her career had stalled, and her marriage was in shambles. Sitting home alone, she found herself wrapped in a blanket of misery, feeling like a failure and angry. She didn't even recognize the person looking back at her in the mirror. She felt like life had done her wrong.

One day while she was journaling, an epiphany struck her. She realized that as long as she saw herself as a victim of life's wrongdoing, that's what she would remain. If she desired change, she needed to transform her perception of herself and her world. She had to step out of her comfort zone, embrace vulnerability, and take personal accountability to achieve this. She wrote a mantra to guide her: "If it has to be, it's up to me." She was responsible for her life's trajectory.

Jo retraced her steps. How did she get to this point? Digging into both her personal history and her personal files, Jo tore into her closet and retrieved a dusty manuscript she had started years ago. Thumbing through the pages of her old self, she felt a revival of childlike enthusiasm. Who was she when she began writing this book? Successful. Driven. Confident. Always up for a challenge.

She flipped through the pages, taking an accounting of her life, and began jotting down her thoughts. Where did she see herself in a year or five? What current patterns weren't working? That answer was clear: stop clinging to comfort in misery. What paths should she continue? She wanted to get back to writing that book. What dreams needed to be revived? It was time to pursue her long-neglected dream of walking the Camino de Santiago.

The decision to walk this five-hundred-mile pilgrimage marked a significant departure from her comfort zone and familiar lifestyle. But she did it: she walked the Walk of Saint James. Over the two months it took, she encountered physical hardships, connected with people from diverse backgrounds, and faced unexpected challenges.

During this transformative journey, Jo made several profound realizations:

- She had played a role in the deterioration of her marriage and needed to take responsibility for it.
- She possessed more strength and resilience than she had ever realized.
- Fearing the unknown is natural, but remaining trapped in the comfort zone was unacceptable.

Jo's journey of personal accountability forced her to confront her insecurities and limitations. Stepping outside her comfort zone granted her a deeper understanding of herself, including a rediscovery of her strengths and dreams. Today, she embraces life anew, owns a successful business, and is on the verge of completing her book. Jo's transformation is a testament to the power of accountability and the willingness to bust out of one's comfort zone.

How did Jo do that? How did she go from a comfortable victim mentality to an energized, edgy, creative, resilient superhero? Her journey required one of those Fierce Conversations—in this case, a conversation with herself. Beginning with that conversation, she took an honest accounting of her current situation, found it lacking, and took accountability for her need to change. She used the Fierce Accountability Model.

WHAT IS FIERCE ACCOUNTABILITY?

I define *Fierce Accountability* as a desire to take responsibility for results, a bias toward solutions and action. It's an attitude—a personal, private, and nonnegotiable choice about how to live your life. Fierce Accountability is about constructing an empowering context for yourself and your organization.

First, take a look at the context you've built for yourself so far. Remember, your context is your construction. The story you tell yourself is in your mind, and you can change your mind. In building our mental contexts, we're always practicing something. It's our choice to practice a victim mentality or accountability.

In victim mode, the belief is "I can't deliver the results I want because of realities outside of my control. The barrier to growth isn't about me, it's about him, her, them, that, the situation. Not my fault."

The accountable stance is "Given my current reality, what do I need to do to create the results, the career, the relationships, and the life I want?"

Accountability is the belief that your fate is indeed up to you. And this mindset is not just a temporary stance but a way of life, a method of continually assessing and acting toward your goals as well as identifying your role in reaching your organization's goals.

Let's be clear: many of the headwinds we face every day are real. Finding the right talent in a tight job market, limited time and budget resources, a micromanaging boss—sound familiar? Fierce Accountability is about looking in the mirror and asking yourself, Given all these headwinds I face, what am I going to do to get different results?

PRACTICE THE ACCOUNTABILITY MODEL

Take yourself through the following self-interview. Look at how a victim mindset creates a context that detaches you from the results. Ask these questions in this order:

1. *Context*—What's a context where I'm taking a victim stance? Where in my life am I telling myself, "I can't, given all these obstacles"?
2. *Assessment*—What evidence have I gathered to support the data I'm paying attention to?
3. *Emotions*—What am I feeling because of this victim situation?
4. *Behavior*—What behaviors have shown up because of my victimhood?
5. *Results*—What results have been created in this context?

Then list the problems and benefits of this victim cycle. How do the problems and benefits weigh out? One benefit might be the comfort of the familiar, as in Jo's story. One problem might be that your current actions aren't leading you to achieve the results you wanted.

Next, consider a context in which you've had great results and are most accountable. Or look at a situation where you felt like a victim but got yourself out of that way of thinking. Ask these questions in this structured order:

- *Context*—What's a context where I'm taking an accountable stance?
- *Assessment*—What evidence have I gathered to support this assessment of my accountability?
- *Emotions*—What am I feeling because of this accountability situation?
- *Behavior*—What behaviors have shown up because of my accountability?
- *Results*—What results have been created in this context?

Weigh the problems against the benefits. If this situation was a truly accountable process, you probably achieved your intended results—or better.

ENCOURAGING ACCOUNTABILITY IN OTHERS

Often as leaders or coaches, you need to encourage accountability in others. You can't force accountability on a person, but you can help them discover it in themselves. People are driven by many factors, such as fear, rewards, or even a manager's overavailability of advice. To effectively support someone to make the choice of accountability, you need to have empathy, curiosity, and a bias toward action. In this way, you help others uncover their potential through greater clarity, improved understanding, and impetus for change.

To help others, make sure you follow good listening practices:

- Listen carefully.
- Let silence do the heavy lifting.
- Give no advice.
- Don't ask leading questions.
- Ask, "What else?" "What else?" What else?"
- Slow the conversation down.
- Be fully present and attentive.
- This is not about you. It's about the person's conversation with themselves.

Then, follow the steps in table 11.1 to coach others.

Table 11.1. The Accountability Model for coaching others

Step	Conversation
1. Identify the issue.	"Where are you feeling stuck? What roadblocks are impeding your forward progress?" Give them time to think about this.
2. Clarify the issue.	"What's going on? How long has it been going on?" Paraphrase to check your perception: "Is the issue _____?" Help this individual discover what the conversation wants and needs to be about.
3. Determine its current impact.	"How is this issue currently impacting you? How about others? The company? What other results is this situation currently producing? As you consider these results, what do you feel?" Continually ask, "What else?" "What else?" "What else?" Help them interrogate their reality.

Table 11.1. Continued

Step	Conversation
4. Determine any future implications.	"If nothing changes, what are the implications? What's likely to happen? What's at stake for you, others, and the company if nothing changes? (What else? What else? What else?) When you consider these possible outcomes, what do you feel?"
5. Examine their personal contribution to the issue.	"What have you contributed to this issue? What part of this issue has your DNA on it?"
6. Describe the ideal outcome.	"When this issue is resolved, what difference will that make? What results will you enjoy? Others? The company? When you contemplate these results, what do you feel?"
7. Commit to action.	"What's the most potent step you could take to move this issue toward resolution? When will you take it? What's going to try to get in your way and how will you get past it? When can you follow up with me?"

Source: Fierce Inc.

RESILIENCE REFRESHER

- Fierce Accountability is a desire to take responsibility for results and a bias toward solution and action. It's an attitude. It's a personal, private, nonnegotiable choice about how to live your life.
- Accountability cannot be legislated or required.
- If it's to be, it's up to me.

CHAPTER 12

MAINTAINING WORK-LIFE BALANCE
NEGOTIATION CONVERSATION MODEL

Be regular and orderly in your life . . .
so that you may be violent and original in your work.

—GUSTAVE FLAUBERT

Have you ever found yourself in front of your work computer screen, dreaming of your quiet backyard or time spent with your life partner? How long has it been since you relaxed in an Adirondack chair with a cold one in one hand and your true love's hand in the other? How long since you cheered your head off at your kid's soccer game, walked the dog, or even went for a checkup at your doctor's? Perhaps you work to live, but does the foundation of you even have a life outside of work? If you had a hard time with those questions, you may be stoking the fires of burnout.

You can even the scales of work-life balance. Imagine your work-life balance fostering time for laughs and mutual support with good friends, regular exercise that makes you feel vibrant, and volunteer opportunities that make your life more meaningful.

That takes negotiation between your work and life selves as well as among your work and life "teams."

What's a Fierce Negotiation? It's a structured conversation between people trying to reach an agreement that yields the best deal and enriches the relationship. It also includes agreements with yourself. Negotiations are pivotal in resolving conflicts and setting boundaries, enabling employees to manage their workload and personal lives effectively. The art of negotiation, exemplified by the search for what we call a *zone of possible agreement*, is vital for fostering a harmonious work environment that respects diverse needs and aspirations, ultimately enhancing work-life balance for all involved.

The Negotiation Conversation Model is a search for a mutual truth and a common path. It is defined as reaching an agreement or compromise through discussion with others. You know you're having a Fierce Negotiation when the following occurs:

- You are speaking in your real voice.
- You are speaking to the heart of the matter.
- You are really asking and really listening.
- You are enriching a relationship.
- You are different when the conversation is over.

And here's a critical point: your work-life balance negotiation may be with yourself.

CASE STUDY: BALANCING THE SCALES

Angela is a dedicated and passionate leader and COO of a large finance company, known throughout the company as a brilliant strategist and a relentlessly hard worker. Her commitment to her job, however, had come at a steep personal cost. She often found herself sacrificing her personal life and well-being for the sake of the company's success.

Long hours at the office, weekend meetings, and endless business trips had affected her health and strained her relationships with family and friends. She hadn't attended her kids' school plays in years. Her blood pressure was through the roof. Angela had reached a point in her life where she yearned for a better work-life balance, not just for herself but also for her team, who were equally devoted to their jobs.

Recently, she received an eye-opening wake-up call when her closest friend, Sarah, had a serious health scare, passing out from exhaustion while meeting with her direct reports. It was a moment of reckoning for Angela as she realized she was on the path to burning out just like Sarah. She knew she needed to make a change, not just for her own sake but for the well-being of everyone around her. It was time to use the Negotiation Model. First, she needed to take personal responsibility for her unbalanced choices. Then, she needed to renegotiate the terms of her work-life balance. So did her colleagues. In fact, the whole culture of her company needed renegotiation.

Angela and her team all needed a new deal with themselves and with each other. This was not a negotiation to determine a winner. They all needed a win-win solution, so their negotiation needed to take place on authentic and mutual terms.

With a newfound determination to transform her life and foster healthier relationships, she embarked on a negotiation journey. She understood that achieving a better work-life balance was about setting boundaries for herself and creating a culture within her company that promoted well-being and productivity in equal measure.

She approached her mission with a clear understanding that the Fierce Negotiation Conversation Model aims to achieve the zone of possible agreement—the sweet spot where a common ground lives, with a range of actions acceptable to both parties. However, she also realized the importance of preparation and not making assumptions about the other party's needs.

As she initiated conversations with her fellow executives, department heads, and employees, Angela put emotional capital at the forefront. She understood that people make decisions emotionally first and then back them up with logic and rationale, so she sought to enrich the relationships by being genuinely interested in the other person's point of view, listening to their viewpoints with complete focus and attention and making sure she clarified her understanding by restating what she had heard from them.

During these conversations, she identified their needs by asking questions such as "What's the most important thing we can accomplish today? What outcomes would you like to see?" She wanted to interrogate the reality of their work-life balance and understand their challenges.

With a better grasp of everyone's needs, Angela and her colleagues began brainstorming solutions. They provoked learning and creativity to develop options to meet all needs and make the deal as appealing as possible for all parties involved. Once they had a possible solution in mind, they tested the waters by asking, "Does this meet your needs?" Fortunately, it did, and they found common ground. They were ready to move forward and implement a new work-life balance strategy for the company.

In the final moments of the negotiation, Angela said, "I think you've answered all of my questions, and I hope I've answered yours. Can you think of any reason *not* to move forward with this agreement?" They had left nothing on the table, and both parties were eager to embrace the new approach to work-life balance. Through her dedication to the negotiation process, Angela enriched her own life and the lives of her colleagues. Her leadership was also defined by her commitment to the well-being of her team.

THE NEGOTIATION CONVERSATION MODEL

No matter what you are negotiating, having a structured and Fierce Negotiation Conversation involves five steps. This means having conversations not only with others but also with yourself. These steps are outlined in the next section.

An important aspect of the Negotiation Model, especially when preparing, is to make sure your listening skills are functioning well. I am fond of acronyms and find this one useful to keep me focused on listening: CLICK—curiosity, listen intently, and clarify knowledge. I think of it as the way to make a relationship click during all structured conversations, and it is especially useful to truly listen to your negotiating partner's story. To make a conversation click, take the following steps:

C: *Curiosity*—Be genuinely interested in what you're hearing.

LI: Listening intently—Be wholly present in that moment of listening, not just waiting for your turn to talk. Turn off your phone.

CK: Clarifying knowledge—Use the "I'm hearing you say that . . ." method of repeating your perceptions to be sure you've understood what they're saying, not just glomming your reality on to theirs.

Learning to listen takes practice. I recommend finding a person who wants to enhance their listening skills and trying this exercise:

1. Take turns as the speaker and the listener.
2. The speaker will discuss their concerns about an upcoming negotiation.
3. The listener applies the CLICK listening tools: Be curious. Listen intently, and be fully present without distraction. Clarify your understanding by rephrasing what you've heard and checking to be sure you've got it right.

Let's turn to the five steps of the Negotiation Model as seen in table 12.1.

PRACTICE THE NEGOTIATION MODEL

What does the Negotiation Conversation Model actually look like? Let's examine what each stage involves.

Preparation

I find looking at the preparation stage through this lens useful:

- *Who*—List the people who have a part in this negotiation. For the work-life balance conversation, you may have your work self talking to your life self. That's okay. Write down names, job titles, whom they report to in the organization, and their decision-making power.
- *What*—What's the need that you have identified? What do you believe your counterpart negotiator is missing in their understanding of the situation? What are they not addressing but need to?
- *When*—When does this decision need to be made? In the work-life balance negotiation, this may mean determining your degree of desperation.

Table 12.1. The Negotiation Conversation Model

Step	Description
1. Prepare.	• What are the symptoms of the problem? • Lay out the scene and the cast of negotiating characters. • Interrogate the reality of these relationships with your negotiation partners. • Look at the emotional landscape.
2. Identify everyone's needs.	• Paraphrase by saying, "If I'm understanding you correctly, what you are telling me is . . ." • Define the problem's current impact. • Determine future implications if nothing changes. • Examine the relevant history. • What are you most concerned about regarding recent history? • Describe the ideal outcome. • Explore creative possibilities.
3. Brainstorm solutions.	• Generate many opinions. • Look for need-blending opportunities. • Identify shared potential beyond the current negotiation. • Listen. Listen some more. • Narrow your options before choosing a solution. • Ask for each solution, "What if this? If this, then what?"
4. Test the waters.	• Perform a needs check. • Does this solution meet your needs? • If yes, go on to closing questions. • If no, listen some more.
5. Close the deal.	• Ask closing questions. • Put it in writing. • Follow up.

Source: Fierce Inc.

- *Where*—Where is this problem coming from in the organization? Where does the solution need to be applied?
- *Why*—Why are you considering this solution?
- *How*—How will they make the decision to accept your solution? In a self-negotiation, how will you gain enough perspective of your situation to decide?

Remember how I said, "The conversation is the relationship" back in chapter 1? As you prepare for this negotiation conversation, examine your relationship between your work and life selves and with the others who have stakes in this work-life balance culture shift. You'll plan your conversation based on your anticipated level of need for trust-building with your negotiation partner. Interrogate the reality of these relationships with them. Which of these statements resonates?

- We have a strong partnership. We're each other's trusted partner.
- This is a strong relationship. My counterpart advocates for me.
- I'm my counterpart's go-to expert on some issues, but we don't have a formal partnership.
- I haven't built trust yet. They are indifferent to me.

Next, look at the emotional landscape. Emotional intelligence is the ultimate communication tool, and negotiation is an emotional business. We make decisions emotionally and then find rationale for them. Where do you rate yourself on the following statements, with one being poor and five being excellent? The closer to a total score of twenty the better. If you didn't score that high, that's okay. You can increase your score with self-awareness and practice.

- I express emotions appropriately.
- I'm calm in the face of strong emotions.
- I'm assertive without damaging my relationships.
- I can enhance the relationship without diminishing results.
- I can listen to questions and learn rather than just reply.

Identifying Needs

In the second step of the Negotiation Conversation Model, you will identify everyone's needs. This process will help you determine and clarify your needs and those of the other party.

Once again, tap into the Mineral Rights Exercise from chapter 7 while considering these elements:

1. Determine the problem's current impact.
   - How is this currently impacting you, other people, and the company?
   - When you consider these results, how do you feel?
2. Determine future implications.
   - If nothing changes, what are the implications?
   - What will happen if it doesn't improve?
   - What will happen if it stays the same?
3. Examine the relevant history.
   - What can you tell me about the situation, and what you have done up to this point?
   - What worked, and what didn't work?
   - What are you most concerned about regarding the situation's recent history?
4. Describe the ideal outcome.
   - Ideally, what would you like to see happen?
   - What does your ideal outcome look like?
   - What would the perfect solution look like to you?

5. Explore creative possibilities.
    - Can we talk about some potential ways to solve this that work for both of us? Without committing to anything yet, let's brainstorm some possibilities.

I find summarizing this in a Needs Assessment Matrix, such as the one in table 12.2, keeps negotiation focused and productive. Where do you and your negotiating partner's needs overlap? That is your zone of possible agreement. That's where you're most likely to find a mutually satisfying solution.

Brainstorming Solutions

The next step in the Negotiation Conversation Model is to brainstorm solutions together. To get the most out of this stage, aim to do the following:

- Generate many opinions.
- Look for need-blending opportunities.
- Identify shared potential beyond the current negotiation.
- Remember to listen.
- Narrow your options before choosing a solution.
- Ask for each solution, "What if this? If this, then what?"

Table 12.2. Needs Assessment Matrix

	My needs	Their needs
Must-haves		
Realistic		
Bonus		

Source: Fierce Inc.

Testing the Waters

Too often, people go straight to closing the deal after brainstorming potential solutions. This is a big mistake. Testing the waters by doing a needs check-in is important at this point. If the solution does not meet both your and your negotiating partner's needs, you need to listen more and then go back to brainstorming. If the solution does meet everyone's needs, you are ready to close the deal.

Closing the Deal

This step of the conversation includes pragmatic actions, such as getting the agreement in writing. Equally important is understanding the need for a continued dialogue to measure success and enrich a strong relationship.

Make sure to say the following when closing the deal:

- "I think you've answered all my questions, and I hope I've answered yours."
- "Can you think of any reason *not* to move forward with this agreement?"

While putting the solutions in writing, note the following:

- It's not a deal until it's in writing.
- Write it out, and check with your negotiating partners.
- Is this how they understood your agreed solution?

Finally, make sure to follow up:

- See what happens.
- Measure the success of the solution.

- The conversation is ongoing and will sustain and enrich the relationship with your partners.

As you negotiate a work-life balance, both in yourself and in your organization, you build Fierce Resilience. Finding work-life balance means finding the zone of possible agreement between life and work needs. Further, this zone you've found among your colleagues is the beginning of an organizational culture with practical policies that sustain that balance.

RESILIENCE REFRESHER

- Finding work-life balance requires negotiation.
- The negotiation may be between your work self and your life self, or you may need to negotiate among your coworkers.
- Fierce Negotiation means finding the zone of possible agreement.
- Start with an assessment of your and your negotiating partner's needs.
- Collectively brainstorm solutions.

CHAPTER 13

RESPONDING TO CHANGE
TEAM CONVERSATION MODEL

To improve is to change, so to be perfect is to have changed often.

—Winston Churchill

In the mid-2000s, Ford was in crisis.[1] The company was hemorrhaging billions of dollars, losing market share, and facing quality challenges from Toyota, Honda, and other international competitors. Morale within the organization was at an all-time low. The future looked bleak.

Alan Mulally, an aerospace engineer and Boeing CEO, was brought in as Ford's CEO in 2006. He inherited a company that was struggling to stay afloat and had been plagued by internal divisions, a lack of transparency, and a culture that discouraged open communication. Ford was flailing in the face of industry change. Mulally's first order of business was to address the dysfunctional team dynamics within Ford and build a culture of collaboration, transparency, and resilience. Whether they knew it or not, the Ford leadership team was on a journey toward Fierce Resilience.

Mulally introduced a unifying vision called "One Ford." He emphasized that the entire organization needed to work together as a cohesive team with a shared purpose. This vision aimed to break down silos, eliminate internal competition, and foster collaboration across departments and geographies by focusing on the following themes:

- *Regular business review meetings*—Mulally instituted a weekly business plan review meeting. In these meetings, all of Ford's top executives gathered to openly discuss the company's performance, issues, and solutions. This created a forum for honest communication and problem-solving, eliminating the practice of hiding problems.
- *Open and supportive leadership*—Mulally and his leadership team encouraged open and honest communication at all levels of the organization. They made it clear that sharing problems was not only allowed but also expected. This led to a more transparent and accountable work culture.
- *Empowerment*—Mulally empowered his team to take ownership of their areas and make decisions. He believed that the people closest to the problems were often best suited to find solutions. This approach encouraged innovation and resilience at all levels of the organization.
- *Resilience amid crisis*—The economic crisis of 2008 hit the auto industry hard, but Ford was one of the few American automakers that didn't need a government bailout. The culture of transparency and collaboration that Mulally had instilled allowed Ford to adapt quickly, make tough decisions, and restructure the company without external assistance.

This attitude adjustment at Ford led to a remarkable turnaround for the company. It not only survived the crisis but thrived. Ford's product quality improved, it introduced successful new models, and it regained market share. The culture of teamwork, openness, and resilience played a pivotal role in this transformation.

Mulally's leadership and the culture of teamwork he fostered at Ford serve as a testament to how effective team interaction leads to resilience in the business world. By breaking down silos, encouraging open communication, and empowering employees, Ford was able to overcome immense challenges and emerge as a stronger and more competitive company.

CHANGE AND TEAMWORK

Like many legacy American manufacturers, the auto industry had become complacent in their global monopoly. These companies saw themselves as the captains of industry; if anything were to change, they would initiate it. But little did they know, the age of American industrial domination was ending. They needed to stand and face the changes. Too comfortable in their top-dog position, they hadn't needed to think about building resilience. But now they did.

Throughout our evolutionary history, change has been synonymous with uncertainty, often signaling danger in unpredictable environments teeming with potential threats. Our ancestors who excelled in accurately predicting outcomes and minimizing risks were the ones who survived and passed on their genes. This relentless pursuit of certainty became hardwired into our brains as a means of survival, leading us to seek stability and avoid ambiguity. In this ancient context, change equated to stress as our brains interpreted it as a potential threat, triggering a physiological response to prepare for action.

In the modern world, this primal drive for certainty still courses through our veins, evident in our relentless pursuit of stable relationships, financial security, and a foreseeable future. Our brains, driven by eons of adaptation, inherently crave certainty as a survival mechanism. When change disrupts this equilibrium, stress emerges as a powerful motivator, compelling us to regain that precious predictive stability. Even when the change is good, embracing it means challenging the very essence of our evolutionary programming.

Harnessing the power of teams for input and feedback is an effective way to help individuals and organizations navigate and embrace change. That's where the Team Conversation Model comes in. This structured conversation model is designed to elicit multiple perspectives of team members during meetings. It's useful in times of change when you want to rally the unique perspectives of the individuals who make up your organization.

At the core of this model is the Beach Ball Meeting. Imagine your organization as a big, striped beach ball. Each person on your team lives on one of those stripes, each with a different view of the whole from that perspective. The Beach Ball Meeting elicits all of those perspectives and asks its members to listen nonjudgmentally. This is reality interrogation at its best. When you're facing change, one perspective is not enough. You need to let your people's multiple realities each have its place at the table. While at that table, you mine the gold that is the minds of your diverse workforce. Like the other conversation models, the Beach Ball Model requires preparation, deep-dive listening, and action.

CASE STUDY: A BEACH BALL MEETING IN ACTION

In 2021, Cassandra was the director of digital strategy at a regional bank that transitioned its back-office staff to remote roles due to the COVID-19 pandemic. The bank had seen a decline in innovation and trust, prompting management to decide it was time for her team to begin returning to the office.

This decision triggered a division within the team. Some team members cherished the traditional office culture, reminiscing about past gatherings, spontaneous watercooler chats, and the camaraderie forged during in-person meetings. Other team members opposed the return to the office. They had grown accustomed to the flexibility of working from home, which allowed them to balance their professional and family lives. They expressed concerns that increased office attendance would result in longer commutes and higher stress levels.

The team's productivity plummeted as the return-to-office date drew near. Cassandra observed the decline in performance and decided to convene a meeting to address these issues. The meeting used the Beach Ball Model. Cassandra knew she had strong opinions about the decision and needed to gain a comprehensive understanding of the complex dynamics and concerns within her team. By listening to all the stripes on the ball—the advocates for returning to the office, those who prefer remote work, and all those somewhere in between—she formulated a more balanced and inclusive approach to respond to the change.

After inviting members of her team, members of HR, and differing executive leaders across the organization who would give her a wide range of perspectives, she prepped for the meeting. At the meeting, she began by thanking everyone for their participation and emphasized the importance of the discussion. Before delving into the discussion, Cassandra had the team review the preparation form she had developed, emphasizing that naming a problem is the first step toward solving it.

She outlined the meeting's ground rules, urging every participant to share their thoughts, diverse perspectives, and differing opinions. She highlighted the need for open dialogue, encouraging those unsure of what to say to consider the question, What would you say if you did know?

The meeting then proceeded with team members sharing their ideas about wellness programs, office redesign, training and skill development, flexible office attendance, mentoring and coaching, and a slew of other topics. The list was extensive, and Cassandra expressed gratitude for their valuable input.

Following this conversation, she asked each team member to answer the question, "What would you do if you were me?" The following themes rose to the top:

- Redesign the office space to enhance collaboration, creativity, and comfort with various work zones.
- Establish regular feedback channels to value and act on employee input.
- Test the return-to-office strategy through a pilot program with a smaller group before implementing company-wide.

Cassandra responded to each suggestion by simply thanking them. Before concluding the meeting, she asked if anyone had anything else to add or emphasize. She then expressed gratitude for the openness and engagement, expressing her readiness to take initial action on piloting the return-to-office strategy with a smaller group of employees, establishing regular feedback channels, and developing a comprehensive change-management plan encompassing communication, training, and support for employees.

She let them know she would update the team on the progress and requested that they write their names on their recommendations in case she had follow-up questions.

THE IMPORTANCE OF PREPARATION

The Beach Ball Meeting uses a preparation form to clearly identify an issue and determine what you want from the group. Table 13.1

Table 13.1. Team Conversation Model

Prompts and examples	Directions
The issue is . . . *The company has made a decision to have employees begin returning back to the office and there's conflict over this change.*	Be concise. In one or two sentences, get to the heart of the issue. Is it a concern, challenge, opportunity, or recurring problem that is becoming more troublesome?
It's significant because . . . *This change impacts innovation and trust within the team. This issue also affects employee satisfaction, work-life balance, and stress levels. If this issue is not resolved, we could be facing future employee engagement and retention issues.*	What's at stake? For example, how does this affect profitability, people, products, services, customers, timing, the future, or other relevant factors? What's the future impact if the issue is not resolved?
My ideal outcome is . . . *To understand and acknowledge the concerns and perspectives of all team members.* *To find a solution that balances the needs of those who prefer working from the office with those who prefer remote work.* *To rebuild trust and camaraderie within the team.*	What results do you want? Be specific.
Here's the relevant background information . . . *Remote was initially successful, but now we're seeing a decline in innovation and trust. Some team members like the traditional office, others prefer remote work. Concerns include longer commutes and higher stress levels.* *Some team members feel undervalued and unappreciated for their efforts.*	Summarize with bullet points the what, why, where, when, how, who, which forces are at work, and what the current status is.

Table 13.1. Continued

Prompts and examples	Directions
What have I done up to this point? *I have conducted one-on-one meetings with team members to gather their feedback and concerns. I have also initiated discussions with HR to explore potential solutions.*	List all the steps you have taken so far.
Options I'm considering . . . *Provide flexible work hours to accommodate commuting and personal needs. Improve communication channels to address concerns and boost morale. Invest in professional development on change management.*	Write out all the options you are considering. Are there ones you are leaning toward?
The help I want from the group . . . *Thoughts and suggestions on the proposed solutions. Thoughts and suggestions of new solutions. Ideas for fostering team unity. Recommendations on addressing concerns.*	What do you want from the group? For example, what about alternative solutions, confidence regarding the right decision, identification of consequences, where to find more information, or a critique of the current plan?

Source: Fierce Inc.

includes the structure, instructions, and example based on Cassandra's story.

HOLDING A BEACH BALL MEETING

The next time you think you need to implement the Team Conversation Model with a Beach Ball Meeting, take the following steps to ensure it goes smoothly.

Preparation

Before your team conversations, be sure you complete the following checklist:

- Write a clear statement of the decision to be made, the strategy to be outlined, the opportunity to be evaluated, or the problem to be solved.
- Invite the people who will be affected or who have perspectives you need to hear, including decision-makers and outside professionals. In the invitation, let everyone know the issue, its significance, and your desire to learn their perspectives.
- Send out any material that should be reviewed before the team conversation. This enables internal processors to prepare and actively participate and ensures all are laser-focused on the objective of the meeting.

During the Team Conversation

Once you are prepared and ready to start the meeting, take the following steps:

1. Thank everyone for coming.
2. Give everyone a copy of the preparation form, and talk it through to quickly focus attention and resources on the topic.
3. Tell your team members that you want to hear their perspectives, especially if they differ from what you see or the direction you are leaning in. Remember, this is about examining multiple realities.
4. Make sure that you hear from each team member. If someone says, "I don't know," ask, "What would it be if you

did know?" If someone says, "I have nothing to add," ask, "What would you add if you did have something to add?" If you are not sure what someone's comment means or the comment seems incomplete, try, "Please say more about that."

5. When you have heard from everyone and the conversation has lost steam, ask each team member to write down a concise answer to this question: What would you do if you were me?

6. Have each person read their advice. Do not respond, except to say, "Thank you."

7. After everyone has read their advice, tell them what you've heard and ask, "Did I miss anything essential?"

8. Thank everyone for their contributions, and tell them what action you are prepared to take and when you will take it.

9. Ask them to write their name on their recommendations and give them to you so that you can follow up with them if you'd like more information. No notetaking is needed by you! In fact, I strongly urge you not to take notes; be fully present in the conversation, staying current with everyone present.

Action

Get back to everyone once you have decided or acted, and let them know the results and next steps.

RESILIENCE REFRESHER

- A time of change is a time of challenge. But remember, challenge is an opportunity to grow.
- Mine the gold that is your diverse team. Gather their multiple perspectives using the Beach Ball Meeting.
- Practice your nonjudgmental listening, your transparency, and your gratitude for their commitment.
- Act, and communicate your decisions to all involved.

CHAPTER 14

BUILDING INCLUSION

ANOTHER USE OF THE TEAM CONVERSATION MODEL

Your assumptions are your windows on the world.
Scrub them off every once in a while, or the light won't
come in.

—ALAN ALDA

We are wired to discriminate. Our brains spend most of their time rapidly categorizing our experiences and building assumptions by taking mental shortcuts to conclusions about the world and how to navigate it. That's how we learn not to put our hands in the fire or fall into an abyss. But it's also how we build habits of making judgments based on surface characteristics.

Our ability to discriminate saves our lives, but it also creates false assumptions that lead us to misjudge others. Alan Alda was talking to college graduates when he said, "Your assumptions are your windows on the world. Scrub them off every once in a while, or the light won't come in." His objective was to point out a key quality of a true adult: you can challenge your own assumptions.

He went on to say, "I hope you'll always make distinctions. A peach is not its fuzz, a toad is not its warts, a person is not his or her crankiness. If we can make distinctions, we can be tolerant, and we can get to the heart of our problems instead of wrestling endlessly with their gross exteriors. And once you make a habit of making distinctions, you'll begin challenging your own assumptions."[1]

What does all this have to do with your quest of promoting diversity and inclusion in the workforce? Everything. Inclusion is a nurtured habit of mind. Remember the Fierce Conversations principle to interrogate your reality? That's what it means to challenge your assumptions. Inclusion is an attitude, and it has to be woven into a company's culture. Inclusion has to be a pattern of action too. It's manifested in the way your organization communicates.

UNDERSTANDING YOUR CONTEXT FILTER

Everything we've learned, experienced, and processed in our lives—all of that is stashed in our arsenal of assumptions. It's our context filter, the lens through which we perceive the world. This lens shapes how we receive and interpret information. We apply these filters every time we evaluate our own standing, gauge certainty and autonomy, and evaluate fairness. Our context filter is a consolidation of our opinions, attitudes, and beliefs, and when held over time, these components solidify into our unchallenged truths, with a capital *T*.

Our context filter serves as the instrument through which we make sense of the world, accepting information that aligns with our established beliefs and dismissing that which does not. Whenever we encounter a new situation, we make judgments about the situation based on our truth. This is the story we tell ourselves, our internal depiction of the world. We generate emotions from that story, and those emotions then drive our behavior.

Building inclusion in the workplace requires a continuous washing of our windows. Interrogate your reality. Recognize the judgments you make based on your context filter. Interrogating your reality requires realizing that the lens through which each person perceives the world is shaped by their unique background, experiences, and beliefs. That is the first step toward building a more inclusive workplace. By embracing this diversity of perspectives, organizations actively work to challenge the solidified capital *T* truths within their corporate culture, making space for open dialogue and the reevaluation of long-held beliefs. This process of introspection and empathy allows for the formation of new stories about inclusion, which in turn generate positive emotions and drive inclusive behaviors that lead to a more welcoming and equitable workplace for all.

Let me be very clear. I am not asking you to justify the attitudes you've built on your context filter. Instead, I am asking you these questions:

- Is your context filter, your perception of the world, working for you?
- Are you holding on to opinions, attitudes, and beliefs that limit your possibilities?
- Are they leading to assumptions and misunderstandings that cost you, your team, and your organization?
- Is your context filter preventing you from experiencing better results?

CASE STUDY: EXAMINING DIVERSITY USING CONVERSATION MODELS

Several years ago, Dijon Evon, a dedicated and passionate professional, was entrusted with a challenging task at his organization.

He was asked to spearhead the creation of diversity and inclusion programming. It was a mandate he wholeheartedly believed in, but as he delved deeper into the project, he encountered obstacles that tested his resolve.

Dijon was determined to make a difference. He started by researching vendors and experts who could provide guidance on fostering inclusion within the workplace. He found abundant resources, but they primarily focused on addressing behaviors. These resources instructed organizations to tell their employees what not to do, emphasizing the *don'ts* of exclusionary behavior. However, Dijon knew from his life experiences that merely telling someone to stop doing something rarely brought about lasting change.

He couldn't shake the feeling of disillusionment that crept over him as he realized that many of these inclusion programs were missing an essential focus: the underlying attitudes and beliefs that drive behavior. Frustration began to build as he attended meetings with executives who professed a commitment to inclusion but demonstrated contradictory, exclusionary actions. Those leaders seemed to be just making lip service to inclusion.

One day, Dijon decided to pause and have a conversation with himself. He asked himself a series of important questions:

- Why was his stress so high?
- How might he perceive the situation through a different lens?
- What aspects were within his control, and what immediate actions could he take?
- What was his context filter?
- What were the context filters of others in the organization?

This period of self-reflection marked a turning point. He chose to pivot in his approach. He realized that to truly foster inclusion, he needed to create a culture in which individuals felt secure sharing their diverse thoughts, opinions, and ideas without fearing exclusion. Dijon understood that psychological safety and inclusion were inseparable concepts. In a psychologically safe environment, people feel comfortable speaking their minds because they believe their contributions will be respected and considered. He needed to cultivate this environment within his organization.

He recognized that inclusion was not just about ticking a box or complying with diversity quotas but instead sending a clear message that all voices mattered and that diverse perspectives were tolerated and actively sought. This affirmation of diversity would help individuals feel secure in expressing themselves, knowing that the organization valued their unique viewpoints as important to collective success.

With renewed energy and determination, Dijon built a program incorporating psychological safety and inclusion. He aimed to encourage individuals to challenge their context filters, the preconceived notions that often clouded their judgment. He integrated honest and open conversations into the work schedule. He made sure every meeting was a Beach Ball Meeting, sharing and valuing multiple perspectives on the issue at hand.

As his new communication program took shape, the company began to transform. An environment emerged where active inclusion thrived, and psychological safety was upheld as a core value. People felt encouraged to challenge their biases, consider alternative viewpoints, and, most importantly, engage in meaningful conversations that pushed the boundaries of their context filters.

In this transformed workplace, the inclusion of diverse perspectives became the norm. Diverse backgrounds, life experiences, and viewpoints converged to foster creativity and innovation. Decisions and solutions were no longer one-sided but were considered from the various angles of the team's rich human resources, leading to more effective decision-making processes. Are they done? No, but through one conversation at a time, the context filters of employees are checked, expanded, and enriched. They are on the path of building a truly inclusive organization.

PRACTICE YOUR FILTERS

In part 1, I talked a lot about self-awareness, particularly of our stress triggers. Checking your context filters is another process of growing self-awareness. Chances are that some of your stress is triggered by expectations distorted by your context filter. Those expectations send you into interactions with assumptions about how the conversation will go, who this person is, and what you have to win or lose in this interaction. You've already excluded many possible paths that conversation might take.

What if you go into that conversation without your filters? Think of a meeting you've had with someone you consider different from you, whether in age, race, social status, or communication style. Before the meeting, did you predict how that person would act?

List your expectations for how you thought that person would behave, what views they might express, and how the meeting would go. Here are some examples:

- "I know this person is going to talk my ear off."
- "This person always pushes their personal agenda, asking for promotions, raises, better job perks."
- "I don't like the way this person talks. Too loud. They have a New York City accent. New York people are pushy and abrupt. I don't like them."
- "This person doesn't like me. I can tell by the way they talk."

- "We're not going to make any progress in this meeting. This person won't listen to me, so I'm not going to listen to them."

Did your nightmares come true? Of course they did. You had them all in the baggage you took in with you going into the conversation. Were you surprised to find that you'd been wrong in your predictions? Great! That means that you didn't let your context filter cloud your vision of the interaction. With that, you're on the path toward inclusive thinking. This journey is all about open-mindedness, genuine curiosity about multiple perspectives, and a willingness to listen and learn.

You'll find that the more you enact the principles of courage, authenticity, and unfiltered attention, the more you'll learn from the people around you—and the more your worldview will grow to include diverse perspectives.

CASE STUDY: AIMING FOR LEADERSHIP DIVERSITY

A major global investment titan was eager to boost leadership diversity. Its leaders were not just talking about it but actively striving to diminish unconscious biases and up their leadership's diversity game. They've done pretty well with gender balance but wanted to up the ante when it came to ethnic diversity.

The firm set a bold goal: ensure 30 percent diversity among its top brass. While it had a diverse group at the lower rungs, the diversity dwindled higher up the ladder. The initiative team concluded that it was not just about hiring diverse talent; it was about holding on to it.

They got to work training their leaders, emphasizing real-time feedback and coaching. The mantra was clear: relationships bloom through candid conversations. They didn't stop there. The training had an essential module on unconscious bias. They knew they had to question their biases and challenge managers to step out of their comfort zone. To promote open communication, they revamped their approach. Instead of dismissing younger employees' concerns, they started asking probing questions, focusing on understanding different viewpoints.

Almost all of their leaders have since undergone this transformative training. The company has seen a marked increase in open dialogue and a newfound appreciation for different perspectives within the company. They have seen a promising uptrend in hiring and promoting minority talents.

PRACTICE THE BEACH BALL MEETING

Let's revisit the Beach Ball Meeting I discussed in the previous chapter since its whole purpose is to elicit diverse perspectives. As Susan Scott says in *Fierce Leadership*, "Stop *talking* about inclusion and engagement and start *including and engaging* in every conversation, every meeting."[2]

As a reminder, the Beach Ball Model envisions the organization as a giant, multicolor-striped beach ball, with each person standing on their own stripe on the sphere. If you picture this, you'll realize that each stripe's vantage point has a different view of the ball. A Beach Ball Meeting format gives equal time and attention to each stripe's narrative of the issue at hand and requires open-mindedness and active, nonjudgmental listening.

I'd like you to take a few moments to design a meeting on inclusion in your own organization. First, do the preparation work using the format shown in table 13.1 in the previous chapter and briefly summarized below:

1. The issue is _____.
2. It's significant because _____.
3. My ideal outcome is _____.
4. Here's the relevant background information: _____

   _____.
5. What have I done up to this point? _____

   _____.
6. Options that I'm considering: _____.
7. The help I want from the group is _____.

Next, follow these steps for your meeting:

1. Brainstorm about the people you need to invite to a discussion of this topic. Think comprehensively of the organization and whom this issue might affect, then invite them to the Beach Ball Meeting.
2. Prepare the invitees. Let them know the topic, its significance, your desire to hear their perspectives about how to solve it, and your expectation that they will come to the meeting prepared to focus their energy and attention on the topic.
3. Hold the meeting. Thank them all for coming.
4. Let everyone know that you want to hear their perspective on the issue, speaking from each unique stripe on the beach ball.
5. Ask clarifying questions. Really listen.
6. Ask each participant to write down their recommendations for action based on the multiple perspectives they've heard. Have each person read their recommendations out loud.
7. Close the meeting by thanking everyone for their contribution. Have each person sign their written recommendations

and hand them in to you. Thank everyone again for their time and contribution.

RESILIENCE REFRESHER

- We make unconscious decisions to include or exclude a person or an idea based on our existing assumptions—our context filters.
- If we genuinely want to know the truth, we must bust through those context filters or interrogate our reality, in the language of the Fierce Conversations principles.
- Organizational members need to feel safe expressing their diverse perspectives and have sound opportunities to become top leaders.
- Leaders model inclusive culture by being authentic themselves.
- Practice inclusive communication with Fierce Conversation models—that essential conversation with yourself and Beach Ball Meetings.

CHAPTER 15

BUILDING CULTURE
VALUES CONVERSATION MODEL

Culture eats strategy for breakfast.

—ANONYMOUS

One in five American workers has left a job due to a toxic work culture. Almost half of current workers have contemplated leaving.[1] You may be one of them. Clearly, we need to deal with this culture crisis. But you might counter with "Culture is a soft, unmeasurable thing. Let's stick to the money measurables." What if I told you that the cost of turnover due to negative workplace culture was $223,000,000 over the past five years?[2] Is that measurable enough for you?

Culture is the invisible yet essential way of an organization. It's the unspoken rules of behavior, the essential moral assumptions behind the business model, and the patterns of communication and silence. It's a conglomerate of how each person sees themselves and others in the social structure of the organization. It's sort of like a collective mental map of the lay of the organizational land: Where do the roads go? Who lives in the highlands, who in the lowlands? How are the communication networks laid out? What languages are spoken? Who gets in on decision-making?

Why them and not others? What are the immigration laws? Who gets in, who gets out? Why? Who decides?

It's fashionable these days for management to try to legislate a fair and inclusive culture by adopting systems like "the five pillars of quality" and such, assuming that the slogans on those break-room posters will trickle down to the hearts and minds of the workers. But we learn from what management *does*, not what they *say*. If management disrespects workers or customers, that fundamental disrespect is woven into the fabric of company culture. *If managers never sit down with their people and have essential and transparent conversations, then communication will happen by hearsay, rumor, and conspiracy. No one feels safe.* If managers say the right thing but do the wrong thing, that behavior is seen as par for the course. It becomes part of the culture.

AN EXAMPLE OF CULTURE FAILURE

Hundreds of people died in Boeing 737 Max plane crashes in 2018 and 2019. It was found that those new planes had been allowed to take to the sky crippled with multiple safety issues and that those safety problems had been allowed to remain and fester during the plane's development. Boeing engineers knew all along that the planes were not ready to fly, but the workplace culture prevented them from speaking the truth to corporate decision-makers.

Why didn't the Boeing engineers speak out? They were afraid for their jobs. Promulgating pressure to meet production deadlines, the company had nurtured in its employees a fear of reprisal for saying anything that might slow production. The engineers expressed concern among themselves but didn't feel safe enough in their place in the organization to speak to the higher-ups.

Dr. Amy Edmondson of Harvard Business School points out the Boeing 737 Max story as "a textbook case of how the absence of psychological safety can lead to disastrous results."[3] Her recommendations to leaders to avoid such disasters all focus on communication. She advocates that leaders need to clearly share the company's financial and market status, solicit input from employees in a respectful, professional, not on-the-spot way, and welcome messengers of opinion regardless of their position or the difficulty of their message.

Dr. Edmondson has promoted this concept of psychological safety as a requisite for healthy organizational culture. She started out studying medical institutions, finding that their hierarchical structure impeded the reporting of errors for fear of reprisal. The workers on the front lines (med students, nurses, and techs) were the first to witness the effects of medical errors as patients suffered and died, but they hesitated to report them to the attending physicians who were their superiors and arbiters of their employment. Those lower down in the organizational culture had learned not to speak up. This culture had one-directional communication. The higher-ups did the talking while the real deliverers of care were not part of the conversation. They didn't feel safe.[4]

COMMUNICATION SKILLS AND PSYCHOLOGICAL SAFETY

What are the top three communication skills to promote psychological safety?

- Active listening
- Vulnerability
- Authenticity

No wonder those top-down communication workplaces, such as Boeing and the medical institutions, failed to learn from or retain their employees. These places didn't have a lot of vulnerability, and they certainly weren't listening. And as they kept the company's true financial status from the employees, they sure were not authentic.

When leaders don't lead the culture in an organization, it causes negative consequences. Culture is essential in shaping employee morale, productivity, and overall success. Without clear direction from leadership, employees may develop their interpretations of what is valued and rewarded, potentially leading to a fragmented and disjointed culture. This results in misalignment between organizational goals and individual actions, fostering a sense of disconnection and frustration among team members.

Ultimately, a lack of leadership in shaping the culture erodes trust, hinders collaboration, and impedes the organization's ability to adapt to changing circumstances. Leaders who don't actively shape the culture risk negative outcomes that have far-reaching consequences. Additionally, toxic behaviors may go unchecked in a culture lacking strong leadership, leading to increased stress, higher turnover, and decreased productivity. A positive and inclusive work environment is essential in attracting and retaining top talent.

Are you building a new culture for a start-up? Or are you determined to take your existing organization's culture from toxic to transformational? In either case, you need to build the foundations of a fierce organization, and that's all about integrating fierce communication practices into the culture. We've seen that resilience is the key to growth, both personal and on the bottom line, beginning with self-awareness and combatting stress through Fierce Conversations. So let's infuse your culture with Fierce Resilience. Raef and Ava's story is a great example of how to do that.

CASE STUDY: **HOW TO GROW A CULTURE**

Business partners Raef and Ava were no strangers to the harsh realities of corporate life, having toiled in environments that thrived on stress, were devoid of meaningful conversations, and were marred by toxic relationships. These experiences left a bitter taste in their mouths, and they knew early on what kind of culture they didn't want. When Raef and Ava embarked on their entrepreneurial journey and founded their own real estate company, they made a pact to intentionally mold its culture.

For them, this meant nurturing deep and authentic relationships with their teams and clients. They understood that people's loyalty to a company often stemmed from emotional bonds, not purely rational decisions. They knew that if their relationships were solely transactional, revolving around exchanging time and talent for a paycheck, their organization would become a revolving door of talent.

Raef and Ava's business was no cakewalk; it operated in a fast-paced and often stressful environment. Leading the culture meant mastering the art of navigating through stress and bouncing back with resilience. They needed to build resilience in themselves to model that resilient culture for their employees.

They started with that most important Fierce Conversation: the conversation with themselves. They used the Values Conversation Model. They clarified their own goals and their goals for their company. They were honest about their fears and the possible barriers to success. They took an honest accounting of their skills and the skills they would need from their staff. But most importantly, they set down what they wanted for their organizational culture. They wanted a culture of engagement, empowerment, and communication.

To achieve their goals, they instituted a practice of honest, face-to-face feedback, 365 days a year, both for praise and for criticism. They used a meeting format in their planning process, where each person involved gets to clarify their perspective and no one perspective rules. They learned and taught how to listen. Essentially, they worked every day to embody the four objectives of every Fierce Conversation, which I talked about in part 1:

- *Interrogate reality*—Allow for multiple perspectives. Assault assumptions. Seek the truth.
- *Provoke learning*—Use difficult times to learn and grow.
- *Tackle tough challenges*—Do what's hardest first. Those challenges are the best sources of learning.
- *Enrich relationships*—Relationships are what it's all about. Cultivate the emotional side of the business relationship, not just the transactional. And the conversation is the relationship. Integrate honest conversation into the ways of the workplace.

One pivotal moment for their company arrived during the grand opening of a new office building, which included a collaborative workspace. The event required the efforts of everyone on their team. The stakes were high, and the stress levels were even higher. Last minute sound checks became a source of chaos, as the microphones kept blowing the power for the entire outdoor setup.

However, the team viewed challenges as opportunities rather than paralyzing setbacks. They remained calm, working together to quickly identify the problem—a power overload at a single junction box. The team had the tech skill and the communication fluency to get the fix done, and the solution was simple: reroute the power source for the microphones. Problem solved. Team strengthened.

Raef and Ava weren't the type of leaders who micromanaged every detail. As evidenced by the microphone fiasco, they had emboldened their entire team to take control. The team understood that their leaders believed in them, fostering a sense of empowerment that allowed them to focus their efforts to make the most significant impact. Instead of feeling helpless or like victims of their circumstances, the team felt a sense of ownership. The event was a massive success, and while mistakes certainly happened along the way, the team adeptly course-corrected and forged ahead when obstacles arose.

What fuels Raef and Ava's dedication to leading the culture is their rich relationships with their team members and their unwavering commitment to their goals. Their original goals included building a healthy organizational culture rich with communicative relationships and mutual support. That commitment gave them a compelling reason to keep pushing, fighting, and setting the tone for their company's culture.

Among their goals for their organizational culture was a healthy work-life balance. Recently, Raef and Ava decided to take the dream vacation they had been putting off for years: thirty days, two kids, five countries, and a lifetime of memories. The team was not nervous or bitter. They knew they could handle any obstacles they came across, and they wanted their leaders to get back the joy they'd brought to others. They saw Raef and Ava modeling work-life balance. Every day, every member of the team knew they could lead the culture. It was ingrained in the fabric of the relationship, stitched together through one conversation at a time.

PRACTICE THE VALUES CONVERSATION MODEL

I have pointed out that the first essential conversation is with yourself. Your task is to model the self-awareness and behavior you want for your organization, so let's start where you are. Drill down into your intrinsic values and interrogate your reality. Write your vision statement. Have a values clarification conversation with yourself by asking yourself these questions:

- Why are you here? Why does this organization need to exist, beyond just making a product or service that people will buy? How do you want your organization to change the world for its employees and the world in general?
- What's your ideal relationship with everyone connected to your organization? What kind of community do you want to foster?
- What's your ideal relationship with your customers—beyond just supplying them with what they want and getting a big margin for you? How do you want to communicate with them? How will you get to know what they need? How will you sustain the relationship?
- What contribution do you want to make to the global community? Beyond growing the global economy, how do you want your organization to change the world?

Next, interrogate your reality. For each of those values you've identified, ask yourself how you've manifested it in your behavior so far. This is the next step in self awareness. You might find that your behavior hasn't totally aligned with your values. That's because you have the attitude of control. Your actions are something that you can control. You can start now.

Once you have had that conversation with yourself, you will have an idea of the kind of values you want to embody for your organization. Those values will be the framework of your culture and undergird how your organization will communicate both within itself and with the outside world.

You'll need to start on the self-awareness part next. If you're starting up a new company, you will build your culture around the communication practices that you establish. Answer these questions:

- How will you lead meetings?
- How will you model day-to-day internal communication?
- How will you provide feedback?
- How will you embrace conflict?
- How will you enrich customer relations?

If you're looking to change the established culture of your organization, make sure to take the slow and careful road of one-on-one Fierce Conversations with each of the folks you work with. Listen. Then, equipped with the intelligence you've gathered, lead. Gradually work Fierce Conversation practices into your meetings, feedback sessions, and day-to-day communication. Keep listening.

CASE STUDY: WHEN A LEADER ENCOURAGES CONVERSATION

Tony Hsieh, the former CEO of Zappos, was not just a business leader; he was a visionary who believed in the power of company culture and the importance of employee happiness.[5]

At Zappos, Hsieh spearheaded an initiative called "The Offer," with the goal of ensuring that employees were genuinely committed to the company's values and culture. If employees felt the culture wasn't a good fit for them, they could leave with a month's salary.

Hsieh brought simpatico employees in with the "Zappos Family Core Values Interview." This involved not only assessing a candidate's skills but also evaluating their compatibility with the company's core values. Hsieh knew that hiring people who were in line with Zappos's values would help build a cohesive and collaborative workplace culture.

An ABC News *Nightline* profile showed Hsieh in his CEO office: a *Dilbert*-size cubicle in the middle of the call center. From his place there on the front lines, Hsieh encouraged employees to share their thoughts and ideas. He created a culture of open dialogue and communication, where everyone's input was not only welcomed but also considered important to the company's success. This approach helped to break down the barriers of hierarchy and empower employees at all levels.

Zappos was known for its exceptional customer service and unique company culture. Hsieh's emphasis on open communication, employee engagement, and a strong company culture played a huge role in the company's success. This example highlights the transformative power of leadership that prioritizes conversation, connection, and a positive work environment.

RESILIENCE REFRESHER

- Building a resilient culture takes time.
- It takes lots of practice, self-awareness, and commitment.
- Most of all, it takes honest and engaged conversations.
- The Values Conversation Model helps everyone get on board so that a values-based culture is built and sustained.

CONCLUSION

I was recently talking with a colleague of mine, Elaine, a seventy-year-old serial entrepreneur who has worked for large corporations and founded and scaled her own successful businesses. Elaine was fifty when the book *Fierce Conversations* was published and going full speed ahead on many fronts. At that time, her three sons were off building their own lives and her parents had some health issues.

Elaine said she was skeptical about reading Susan's book, but her mentor and a facilitator in an international women's business mentoring organization had strongly recommended it to her chapter members. "I remember doing an eye roll. Not on my list of things to do in my very busy life. Besides, I knew how to have a conversation. My ability to talk with people was one of my biggest assets."

She told me the book had a profound effect on her. It improved her work and leadership. She became a better mother and wife. I asked her to read the draft of *Fierce Resilience*. I was a little worried because, to be honest, Susan Scott is a hard act to follow.

"You've got an important book here, Ed," she said to me. "I really never thought of resilience in this way. I thought it was a character trait, not a learned skill and mindset."

She went on to say that while she has mellowed as she has grown older, in many ways, stress has increased. Losing friends. More worries about money. Concerns about health. Moving to a new area. Transitioning businesses. "This book really helped me see that I can use what I learned in *Fierce Conversations* to have productive conversations about the big and little things that are stressing me out. But what I really loved was that getting tuned to my body through biometric intelligence would help me get at the root causes."

I am grateful for Elaine's perspectives. And I want to hear yours too. I'd love to create a Fierce Resilience movement that reenergizes business, people, and even our countries. Just imagine if decisions started being made in thoughtful ways instead of under stress. The world would simply be a better place.

I would like to leave you with these ten takeaway points as you journey into Fierce Resilience:

- Fierce Resilience is the proactive approach to tackling stress, not just as an individual reaction but by addressing the root causes in our relationships and interactions.
- Traditional resilience training primarily focuses on individual coping mechanisms, often unintentionally perpetuating the victim narrative.
- The primary sources of stress, more often than not, lie in human relationships and our perceptions of those interactions.
- Fierce Resilience bridges the gap between an individual and their stressor, emphasizing the critical role of effective conversations.
- Structured conversations are essential in bringing about resolutions between the individual and the stress source.
- Beyond the individual, organizations can institutionalize Fierce Resilience by promoting healthy conversations within their cultures.

- The detrimental effects of stress are undeniable, impacting not only individual health but also organizational performance and profitability.
- Through coaching and training, it's evident that stress stems largely from miscommunications or misperceptions in human interactions.
- Addressing stress requires a deep self-awareness of personal triggers and understanding the impact of one's actions on others. Modern biometrics assist in identifying these triggers.
- Fierce Conversations are the key—a structured dialogue that unravels misunderstandings and directly addresses the root of the stress, fostering both personal and organizational growth.

NOTES

CHAPTER 1

1. D. E. Alexander, "Resilience and Disaster Risk Reduction: An Etymological Journey," *Natural Hazards and Earth System Sciences* 13, no. 11 (November 5, 2013): 2707–2716, doi.org/10.5194/nhess-13-2707-2013.

2. Stephen Southwick et al., "Resilience Definitions, Theory, and Challenges: Interdisciplinary Perspectives," *European Journal of Psychotraumatology* 5, no. 1 (October 2014), doi.org/10.3402/ejpt.v5.25338.

3. Southwick et al., "Resilience Definitions."

4. "Resilience," Psychology Topics, American Psychological Association, May 2022, apa.org/topics/resilience.

5. "Bouncing," Superpower Wiki, March 4, 2024, powerlisting.fandom.com/wiki/Bouncing.

6. Janet Ledesma, "Conceptual Frameworks and Research Models of Resilience in Leadership," *Sage Open* 4, no. 3 (August 2014), doi.org/10.1177/2158244014545464.

7. Suzanne Kobasa, "Stressful Life Events, Personality, and Health: An Inquiry into Hardiness," *Journal of Personality and Social Psychology* 37, no. 1 (1979): 1–11, doi.org/10.1037/0022-3514.37.1.1.

8. Salvatore Maddi and Deborah Khoshaba, *Resilience at Work* (New York: MJF Books, 2005).

9. Salvatore Maddi, "Hardiness Training at Illinois Bell Telephone," in *Health Promotion Evaluation*, ed. Joseph P. Opatz (Stevens Point, WI: National Wellness Institute, 1987), 101–115.

10. "Highlights: Workplace Stress and Anxiety Survey," Anxiety and Depression Society of America, September 22, 2021, adaa.org /workplace-stress-anxiety-disorders-survey.

11. Susan Scott, *Fierce Conversations* (New York: Berkley Books, 2002), 7.

CHAPTER 2

1. Kevin Dickinson, "The World Must Learn from 'Karoshi,' Japan's Overwork Epidemic—before It's Too Late," Big Think, January 23, 2023, bigthink.com/the-learning-curve/karoshi.

2. Frank Pega et al., "Global, Regional, and National Burdens of Ischemic Heart Disease and Stroke Attributable to Exposure to Long Working Hours for 194 Countries, 2000–2016: A Systematic Analysis from the WHO/ILO Joint Estimates of the Work-Related Burden of Disease and Injury," *Environment International* 154 (September 2021), doi.org/10.1016/j.envint.2021.106595.

3. "Workplace Stress Program," American Institute of Stress, September 6, 2023, stress.org/workplace-stress-program.

4. "Stress—Definition and Types," Byju's, accessed January 2, 2023, byjus.com/physics/stress.

5. Rosemary Ricciardelli et al., "'It's Frustrating. . .I Didn't Join to Sit behind a Desk': Police Paperwork as a Source of Organizational Stress," *International Journal of Police Science & Management* 25, no. 4 (August 2023): 516–528, doi.org/10.1177/14613557231188578.

6. Sarah Bond and Dr. Gillian Shapiro, *Tough at the Top? New Rules of Resilience for Women's Business Success*, For Business Sake Consulting, November 2014, forbusinessake.files.wordpress.com/2014/11/tough_at _the_top.pdf.

7. Siang Yong Tan and A. Yip, "Hans Selye (1907–1982): Founder of the Stress Theory," *Singapore Medical Journal* 59, no. 4 (April 2018): 170–171, doi.org/10.11622/smedj.2018043.

8. "Questions and Answers: Stress," World Health Organization, February 21, 2023, who.int//news-room/questions-and-answers/item /stress.

9. Rob Cross and Karen Dillon, "The Hidden Toll of Microstress," *Harvard Business Review*, February 7, 2023, hbr.org/2023/02/the-hidden-toll-of-microstress.

10. Rajendra Acharya et al., "Heart Rate Variability: A Review," *Medical and Biological Engineering and Computing* 44 (November 2006): 1031–1051, doi.org/10.1007/s11517-006-0119-0.

11. Diane A. Kelly, "How Stress Impacts the Brain and Body," BrainFacts.org, October 28, 2022, brainfacts.org/brain-anatomy-and-function/body-systems/2022/stress-the-brain-and-body-102822.

12. "What Doesn't Kill You Makes You Stronger," Dictionary.com, accessed January 2, 2024, dictionary.com/e/slang/what-doesnt-kill-you-makes-you-stronger/.

13. Merilee Kern, "What Is the True Cost of Work-Related Stress?" American Institute of Stress, April 20, 2022, stress.org/what-is-the-true-cost-of-work-related-stress.

14. *State of the Global Workplace: 2023 Report* (Washington, DC: Gallup, 2023), gallup.com/workplace/349484/state-of-the-global-workplace.aspx.

15. Kern, "True Cost of Work-Related Stress."

16. "Workplace Stress," Occupational Safety and Health Administration, accessed January 2, 2024, osha.gov/workplace-stress.

17. Julie Ray, "Global Rise in Unhappiness Stalls," Gallup, June 27, 2023, news.gallup.com/poll/507725/global-rise-unhappiness-stalls.aspx.

18. "Center for Workplace Mental Health," American Psychiatric Association Foundation, accessed December 17, 2023, apafdn.org/impact/workplace/center-for-workplace-mental-health; Ben Wigert, "Employee Burnout: The Causes and Cures," Gallup, August 2, 2023, gallup.com/workplace/508898/employee-burnout-causes-cures.aspx; and Johanna Duffett and Venessa Hughes, "Addressing Burnout in the Workplace," Catalyst: Workplaces That Work for Women, May 13, 2022, catalyst.org/research/burnout-topic-overview.

19. Marilyn Macik-Frey, James Campbell Quick, and Debra L. Nelson, "Advances in Occupational Health: From a Stressful Beginning to a Positive Future," *Journal of Management* 33, no. 6 (December 2007): 809–840, doi.org/10.1177/0149206307307634.

20. Edward J. Bernacki, "Presidential Remarks," American College of Occupational and Environmental Medicine Annual Conference, Chicago, 2002.

21. Elizabeth McNulty, "Improving Nursing Leadership Communication: Fierce Conversations Training," *Clinical Journal of Oncology Nursing* 27, no. 3 (May 2023): 255–258, doi.org/10.1188/23 .CJON.255-258.

22. "Stress in America: A Nation Recovering from Collective Trauma," American Psychological Association, November 2023, apa .org/news/press/releases/stress/2023/collective-trauma-recovery.

23. L. K. Kachadourian et al., "Mindfulness as a Mediator between Trauma Exposure and Mental Health Outcomes: Results from the National Health and Resilience in Veterans Study," *Psychological Trauma: Theory, Research, Practice, and Policy* 13, no. 2 (2021): 223–230, doi.org /10.1037/tra0000995.

24. *2023 Workplace Learning Report: Building the Agile Future*, LinkedIn Learning, accessed January 2, 2024, learning.linkedin.com /resources/workplace-learning-report.

CHAPTER 3

1. Tasha Eurich, "What Self-Awareness Really Is and How to Cultivate It," *Harvard Business Review*, January 4, 2018, hbr.org/2018/01/what -self-awareness-really-is-and-how-to-cultivate-it.

2. Tasha Eurich, "Working with People Who Aren't Self-Aware," *Harvard Business Review*, October 19, 2018, hbr.org/2018/10/working -with-people-who-arent-self-aware.

3. Kirk Warren Brown and Richard M. Ryan, "The Benefits of Being Present: Mindfulness and Its Role in Psychological Well-Being," *Journal of Personality and Social Psychology* 84, no. 4 (2003): 822–848, doi.org /10.1037/0022-3514.84.4.822.

CHAPTER 4

1. Kirk Warren Brown and Richard M. Ryan, "The Benefits of Being Present: Mindfulness and Its Role in Psychological Well-Being," *Journal*

of Personality and Social Psychology 84, no. 4 (2003): 822–848, doi.org
/10.1037/0022-3514.84.4.822.

2. "The Future of Workplace Wellness: Harnessing the Power of
Biofeedback," Emotai, February 9, 2023, www.emotai.tech/blog/the
-future-of-workplace-wellness-harnessing-the-power-of-biofeedback.

3. Robert P. Hirten et al., "A Machine Learning Approach to
Determine Resilience Utilizing Wearable Device Data: Analysis of an
Observational Cohort," *JAMIA Open* 6, no. 2 (May 2023), doi.org
/10.1093/jamiaopen/ooad029.

CHAPTER 5

1. Kieran C. R. Fox et al., "Is Meditation Associated with
Altered Brain Structure? A Systematic Review and Meta-Analysis of
Morphometric Neuroimaging in Meditation Practitioners," *Neuroscience
& Biobehavioral Reviews* 43 (June 2014): 48–73, doi.org/10.1016/j
.neubiorev.2014.03.016.

2. Yi-Yuan Tang, Britta K. Hölzel, and Michael I. Posner, "The
Neuroscience of Mindfulness Meditation," *Nature Reviews Neuroscience*
16, no. 4 (2015): 213–225, doi.org/10.1038/nrn3916.

3. David Gelles, "At Aetna, a C.E.O.'s Management by Mantra," *New
York Times*, February 27, 2015, nytimes.com/2015/03/01/business
/at-aetna-a-ceos-management-by-mantra.html.

4. Larissa Bartlett et al., "A Systematic Review and Meta-Analysis of
Workplace Mindfulness Training Randomized Controlled Trials," *Journal
of Occupational Health Psychology* 24, no. 1 (February 2019): 108–126,
doi.org/10.1037/ocp0000146.

5. James Rumbold, David Fletcher, and Kevin Daniels, "A
Systematic Review of Stress Management Interventions with Sport
Performers," *Sport, Exercise, and Performance Psychology* 1, no. 3 (2012):
173–193, doi.org/10.1037/a0026628.

6. Rajpal Brar, "Explained: Why LeBron James Meditates during
Games," SB Nation, March 1, 2022, silverscreenandroll.com/2022
/3/1/22950370/why-lebron-james-meditates-during-games-explained
-lakers-video-breakdown.

7. Sara Algoe et al., "A New Perspective on the Social Functions of
Emotions: Gratitude and the Witnessing Effect," *Journal of Personality and*

Social Psychology 119, no. 1 (2020): 40–74, saraalgoe.com/_files/ugd /30fbd7_d855562d5eac426c89fa9243b628f4d5.pdf.

8. Mark Le Fevre, Jonathan Matheny, and Gregory S. Kolt, "Eustress, Distress, and Interpretation in Occupational Stress," *Journal of Managerial Psychology* 18, no. 7 (November 2003): 726–744, doi.org /10.1108/02683940310502412.

9. Clarke Stout et al., "Unusually Low Incidence of Death from Myocardial Infarction: Study of an Italian American Community in Pennsylvania," *JAMA* 188, no. 10 (1964): 845–849, doi.org/10.1001 /jama.1964.03060360005001.

CHAPTER 6

1. Peg C. Neuhauser, *Corporate Legends and Lore: The Power of Storytelling as a Management Tool* (Chicago: McGraw-Hill, 1993).

2. Jerome Bruner, *Actual Minds, Possible Worlds* (Cambridge, MA: Harvard University Press, 1986).

CHAPTER 8

1. Susan Scott, *Fierce Leadership: A Bold Alternative to the Worst "Best" Practices of Business Today* (New York: Crown Business, 2009), 15.

2. Caitlin Mazur, "20 Essential Employee Feedback Statistics [2023]: Employees Want More Than Just Performance Reviews," Zippia, February 1, 2023, zippia.com/advice/employee-feedback-statistics.

CHAPTER 9

1. Vanessa Rose, "Workplace Relationships Stats: How Relationships Affect Engagement and Stress," Pollack Peacebuilding Systems, October 20, 2019, pollackpeacebuilding.com/blog/workplace-relationships-stats.

CHAPTER 10

1. Indra Nooyi, *My Life in Full: Work, Family, and Our Future* (New York: Portfolio, 2021).

CHAPTER 11

1. G. R. J. Hockey, "Yerkes-Dodson law," in *Encyclopedia of Human Behavior*, ed. V. S. Ramachandran, 2nd ed., vol. 4 (Boston: Academic Press, 2013), 767–770.

CHAPTER 13

1. Bryce G. Hoffman, *American Icon: Alan Mulally and the Fight to Save Ford Motor Company* (New York: Crown Business, 2012).

CHAPTER 14

1. Alan Alda, *62nd Commencement Address* (Connecticut College Digital Commons, June 1, 1980), digitalcommons.conncoll.edu /commence/7.
2. Susan Scott, *Fierce Leadership: A Bold Alternative to the Worst "Best" Practices of Business Today* (New York: Crown Business, 2009), 170.

CHAPTER 15

1. "2023 Work in America Survey," American Psychological Association, accessed January 2, 2024, apa.org/pubs/reports/work-in -america/2023-workplace-health-well-being.
2. "SHRM Reports Toxic Workplace Cultures Cost Billions," Society for Human Resource Management, September 25, 2019, shrm.org/about /press-room/shrm-reports-toxic-workplace-cultures-cost-billions.
3. Amy C. Edmondson, "Boeing and the Importance of Encouraging Employees to Speak Up," *Harvard Business Review*, May 4, 2019, hbr .org/2019/05/boeing-and-the-importance-of-encouraging-employees -to-speak-up.
4. Gabrielle Redford, "Amy Edmonson: Psychological Safety Is Critically Important in Medicine," AAMC News, November 12, 2019, aamc.org/news/amy-edmondson-psychological-safety-critically -important-medicine.
5. Sarah Johnson, "Open Communication and Employee Engagement at Zappos under Tony Hsieh," *Harvard Business Review*, May–June 2019, 45–53.

ACKNOWLEDGMENTS

This book would not have been possible without the direct and indirect support of so many. First, thank you, Kathy Palokoff and Janet Heyneman, for keeping our project on track, for keeping me accountable and sane, and for your excellent ideas and contributions to this book. Your belief in the project from day one was my inspiration. There would be no book without you.

Gabe De La Rosa, whom I have known since high school, brought tremendous expertise, research, passion, and collaboration to our innovation, products, and delivery, much of which is captured in this book. You are awesome, man, and I can't even begin to measure the value of our friendship.

The Fierce folks, clients, and advisers responsible are numerous. I had the privilege of leveraging such impactful content and delivery that has evolved and been perfected over many years from the core creation of Susan Scott. To Geeta, who has believed in me and our vision from day one. There would be no Pulse without you and your ability to make the impossible possible. I appreciate your running with me always.

This was a team effort; many have provided expertise, content, and reviews to keep us consistent with the great foundation created by so many at Fierce. To name two, Chantell Brandt and Joe Parent. To all of you, thank you.

To Neal, Jeevan, and the team at Berrett-Koehler, I appreciate your belief in the project and expertise. Thank you, Leticia Gomez, founder of Savvy Literary, for being the most excellent agent and knocking it out of the park for us.

Last, I thank my wonderful wife, who supported and believed in me when I didn't have a clear line of sight into what was possible. I appreciate your giving me the room to get all this done, especially during the holidays. Your turn is next!

To my boys and future generations, know that anything is possible. Think of life as a swimming pool; you are feeling your way through it. If you put your work in mentally, physically, and spiritually every day, you won't go wrong. Special callout to the previous generations who put real work in and are the ones on whose shoulders I stand.

I leave you with one of my favorite quotes by Frederick Douglass that accurately captures the lens of how I see life: "[People] might not get all they work for in this world, but they must certainly work for all they get."

Thank you, readers.

INDEX

ABOUT THE AUTHOR

 As CEO of Fierce Inc., Edward Jason Beltran has led the global company to become one of the most innovative firms in communication and leadership training by rolling out three-dimensional training, metaverse initiatives, and multiple apps. His mission is simple: to impact as many lives and better the world one conversation at a time.

Ed's initiatives are designed to take the company into the future of corporate training and beyond, built on a twenty-year foundation by Susan Scott, company founder and author of the iconic book *Fierce Conversations*. Fierce offers a comprehensive range of training programs, coaching services, and consulting solutions to develop open and authentic dialogue within businesses, enabling leaders and teams to enhance their communication skills, build stronger relationships, and drive positive organizational change.

In 2017, he came onboard the company as the CFO responsible for digital transformation, and as CEO in 2020, he pivoted the organization on three pillars: sustainability, scale, and application. With this foundation, he brought in cutting-edge science around resilience, stress management, and artificial intelligence. The culmination of this new focus resulted in Pulse by Fierce, which marries biometric intelligence with structured conversations to provide real-time feedback, data-driven insights, and personalized learning pathways.

Passionate about [illegible] innovation to improve leadership and companies, Ed [illegible]ogy enthusiast and sees huge applications from artificial [illegible]ence advances.

As an industry thought leader and architect of the Pulse platform, Ed harnessed biometric intelligence to provide people with deep self-awareness of stress factors based on their body's reaction to their environment, followed by productive and successful actions. The results from this have positively impacted people around the globe.

A disruptive innovator throughout his career with a track record of infusing technology innovation to processes and products, Ed has driven hundreds of millions of dollars in incremental revenue and enterprise value. Before joining Fierce, he held executive positions in large multinational organizations, such as Agilent Technologies, Avnet Inc., PricewaterhouseCoopers, and Arthur Andersen.

Ed has an MBA from the Ross School of Business at the University of Michigan and certificates in programs from Wharton and Harvard. He holds multiple bachelor's degrees from Arizona State University in accountancy and computer information systems. He has contributed to CNBC, *Fortune, Wall Street Journal, Forbes, Fast Company,* and HR.com, where he also serves on its advisory board.

Born and raised in San Jose, California, Ed now resides with his wife and two sons in Phoenix, Arizona. He and his wife grew up together and attended Catholic elementary school on the east side of San Jose. He is an avid cycling enthusiast, riding over one hundred miles a week year-around.

A SPECIAL OFFER FOR *FIERCE RESILIENCE* READERS

Thank you for reading *Fierce Resilience*. As a thank you, we would like to offer you Pulse, a proven application designed to redefine how to deal with stress, enhance resiliency, and increase productivity.

Pulse seamlessly connects with smartwatches to provide a timeline of your stress triggers based on biometric intelligence. By addressing unique triggers with our proven strategies, Pulse strengthens resiliency, reduces stress, and prevents burnout before it begins.

Here are some key features:

- Resiliency Timeline: Track hourly stress levels to identify patterns and triggers.
- Evidence-Based Results: Utilize proven strategies to reduce stress.
- Personalized Action Plan: Leverage biometric intelligence to enhance resiliency.
- Embrace your future with Pulse. Take action.
- Scan below to claim your special offer.

Dear reader,

Thank you for picking up this book and welcome to the worldwide BK community! You're joining a special group of people who have come together to create positive change in their lives, organizations, and communities.

What's BK all about?

Our mission is to connect people and ideas to create a world that works for all.

Why? Our communities, organizations, and lives get bogged down by old paradigms of self-interest, exclusion, hierarchy, and privilege. But we believe that can change. That's why we seek the leading experts on these challenges—and share their actionable ideas with you.

A welcome gift

To help you get started, we'd like to offer you a **free copy** of one of our bestselling ebooks:

www.bkconnection.com/welcome

When you claim your **free ebook**, you'll also be subscribed to our blog.

Our freshest insights

Access the best new tools and ideas for leaders at all levels on our blog at ideas.bkconnection.com.

Sincerely,

Your friends at Berrett-Koehler

Certified

Corporation

MIX
Paper | Supporting
responsible forestry
FSC® C016245